...il
...om Mum & Dad.
Christmas '75.

Peter Devlin

Range Rider

Frederick Muller books by Paul Buddee include:

AIR STORIES
Air Patrol and the Hijackers
Air Patrol and the Saboteurs
Air Patrol and the Secret Intruders
Air Patrol and the Underwater Spies

PONY CLUB STORIES
Ann Rankin and the Boy Who Painted Horses
Ann Rankin and the House on Coolabah Hill
Ann Rankin and the Lost Valley
Ann Rankin and the Great Flood

OUTBACK STORIES
Peter Devlin Fights for Survival
Peter Devlin—Range Rider
Peter Devlin—Buffalo Hunter
Peter Devlin and the Road Bandits

Other Titles:

Osca and Olga
Rupert and Rita
Rattigan Rat
The Unwilling Adventurers
The Mystery of Moma Island
The Escape of the Fenians
The Escape of John O'Reilly
Stand To and Other War Poems

Peter Devlin

Range Rider

PAUL BUDDEE

FREDERICK MULLER
LONDON

First published in Great Britain in 1973
by Frederick Muller Ltd., London

ISBN 0 584 96990 2

Contents

1	Introduction to Some Places and People	11
2	Yullamooloo Plains	18
3	Plenty of Opening for Error	31
4	Meet Les Stewart	42
5	The Wool-Bale Loader	56
6	Stations Are Not What They Used To Be	70
7	Click Go the Shears	79
8	Some Lessons from the Expert	96
9	Jet Jacks Up	100
10	Joe Wilson Reads the Lesson	114
11	All Work and Some Play	121
12	The Great Match	131
13	The Goat Business	139
14	The Mysterious Mr Symon	146
15	Short, Sharp, but Important	156
16	Jet Disappears	159
17	Which Way, Jet?	165

I am deeply grateful to many people who provided background material for the Peter Devlin series. Mr and Mrs Les Schubert and family of Yallalong made it possible for me to gain first-hand information in regard to the running of a modern station. Mr E. A. Wright of Hancock and Wright opened the way for me to explore the great areas in which he and his remarkable partner have been involved. Mr Ken McCamey, the partners' area manager, gave me much of the bushcraft information for this series. Mr Colin Bielski, liaison officer of Hamersley Iron Pty Ltd, supplied me with much on-the-spot material at Mount Tom Price. My old friend, Stuart Buchan, provided me with much unusual material for this series.

The Westralian Flight School gave me valuable assistance in producing the *Air Patrol* series, and again in this series I am indebted to a staff member, Mr Greg Martin, for flight data. Mr A. D. Sieber of the Nature Advisory Service of the W.A. Education Department was also of great assistance in giving information regarding survival in the desert.

To my wife and Mrs D. V. Bremner I wish to pay tribute for their revision of all that I have written in this series, as well as in the *Air Patrol* and the *Ann Rankin* books.

Chapter One

INTRODUCTION TO SOME PLACES AND PEOPLE

HARRY STEWART HAD ONLY one complaint about the metric system—he could no longer boast that Yullamooloo Plains was a million acres in area. To him, 404,686 hectares did not seem half as impressive.

Nevertheless, no matter what measure was used, Yullamooloo still covered a vast area of country. With its 200 windmills, its 1000 kilometres of fences, its 500 kilometres of roads, its 40 000 sheep, and its huge herd of cattle, it was a place of which to be proud.

Harry Stewart was not a station man, born and bred. Indeed, if it had not been for the war, he might still have been living in the city, serving on the committees of various sporting organisations, or being patron of his old football club, to which he had once brought such glory. In his day he had been the best Australian Rules player in the State.

Perhaps it was the Japanese bullet which had changed his whole way of life. He had cursed at the time, when he knew that he would never again take an active part on a football field. However, it had been this knowledge which had weaned him away from the city, after the war was over, and led him to the success he had made of his many properties, until now he had the ultimate in farming—this great tract of land called Yullamooloo Plains.

He was a kindly man to all who knew him, but he had not achieved success without demanding standards which few achieved, and fewer maintained.

His large family had now grown up and were living their lives according to their dispositions and abilities. One son had become a successful engineer and was occupying an important position abroad, two daughters were married, while Tim and Les, the two youngest of his children, feeling themselves quite capable of standing up to the demands their father made on them, had elected to remain and assist him on his property.

Harry Stewart deplored the fact that the country lost most of its young folk to the big cities. It was therefore refreshing to him, while watching Daniel Creek's Junior Team play a football match one Saturday afternoon, to have his friend, Jack Williams, point out a city lad, Peter Devlin. Peter had reversed the trend, and had come from the city to work on a station.

The boy, according to Williams, had had a run of bad luck to date, his earlier experiences on the land not being very encouraging. However, as he seemed a likely sort of lad, Stewart allowed Williams to persuade him to employ Peter at Yullamooloo Plains.

The boy's father, it appeared, was a prisoner of war in Hanoi, and his mother had left him.

"Devlin has become pretty attached to a part-Aboriginal boy, Jet Mercedes Benz, who has thrown in his lot with him," Williams explained. "They've both got the makings of very fine footballers."

Stewart rose to the bait and agreed to take Jet as well, while Williams, seeing his advantage, added a proviso that he expected both boys to be allowed to come to town to play in the football team. Harry Stewart good-naturedly agreed. Both Peter Devlin and Jet, on hearing of their good fortune in being accepted to work at Stewart's station, were delighted.

Peter was a well-built, good-looking lad of fifteen. Tall for his age, he had an oval face, a rather pointed nose and a mass of unruly brown hair. His months of working under very primitive conditions on Josiah McMichael's station at Boolgana Downs* had strengthened the set of his jaw, and toughened the fibre of his muscles.

* See *Peter Devlin Fights For Survival*

Jet was a year or so younger than Peter. He had been brought up by a white foster-mother for his first eleven years. On her death, his life had completely changed, when he had been successfully reclaimed by his Aboriginal father. The members of his father's tribe had then initiated him into manhood by the full tribal ritual.

When Peter had first met him, many months before, Jet had fully identified himself with his father and his Aboriginal relatives, and had considered himself very much the superior of Peter. A number of misadventures together had then cemented a friendship, which neither boy now wanted to break.

Jet was a handsome lad, tall, lithe, and fine-featured. His future lay in how he resolved the conflict between his two worlds.

Jack Williams and his wife had befriended both boys when they had arrived at the town of Daniel Creek, on the request of an old shearer, Joe Wilson, Williams' batman during the second World War. The boys had been kept busy at the hotel and motel that Williams owned, but it was a relief to Williams to pass them on now to Stewart.

"This is no life for two nice kids like you," he said. "You've worked well and earned your pay and I'll always speak up for you, but you have good prospects with Harry, and indeed in this town, if you keep playing good football.

"You are to go out with Harry after the match next Saturday. In the meantime, Mrs Williams and I will kit you up for the job. They do things in style at the station, and we can't have you looking like two ragamuffins."

"Heck, Mr Williams," said Peter Devlin, "I'm going to be spending the rest of my life paying back all the money people have lent me over the last few months—Mrs Sloan for the fare from the city and some pocket money later, Joe Wilson for twenty dollars so that I could get here, and now you and Mrs Williams for clothing."

Jack Williams laughed.

"I think it's a good thing that you should pay any money you owe. It's an important principle, Peter, but I don't think any of us will be putting the squeeze on you, in the meantime anyway. We'll keep you up to it after you've earned a bit, don't worry."

For the boys it was a pleasure to have good clothes again. Jet, caught up by the excitement, decided that a new pair of jeans, a blue coat, and some bright red shirts might not go amiss, but he insisted on buying these with his own money.

Peter bought some jeans, a black leather jacket, and some purple shirts.

"I'll get you some boots that come high over

your ankles," suggested Williams. "Leggings are much too hot for this country, but as you have probably found out, the spinifex is pretty sharp, and boots give you some protection."

Peter could not but agree. He was still digging from his legs small pieces of the bush which had become embedded weeks before.

It was at this stage that Jet appeared to have a problem, but it was a few days before he explained it to Peter.

"It's my name, Jet Mercedes Benz."

"What's wrong with it?"

"It's not my real name. My ma in the city called me John—I was John Haynes, but when my father got me, they gave me a tribal name, which is nobody's business because it's secret. I suppose my real name is Windmill, after Dad, but that's just as stupid."

"I like the name Jet," said Peter. "Why change all your name? Jet Mercedes without the Benz bit on the end sounds pretty classy to me and a good name too."

"You really think so?"

"Sure. People round here will get to know you, and that's as good a name as any I know."

This seemed to please and satisfy Jet.

"You really intend to make a break and come with me," Peter said. "What do you think your dad will feel about it?"

"Whatever I do will be all right with him.

He says the chips are down, once I leave him, and I'll be able to make my own way without him spoiling it for me."

"We've both got problems," said Peter. "I hope everything works out for both of us."

"I don't see why not; we're not ning-nongs," replied Jet. Which summed the situation up very well.

Chapter Two

YULLAMOOLOO PLAINS

PETER AND JET WERE PLAYING in the curtain-raiser for the senior match of the day on the following Saturday. Full of enthusiasm, in the light of their recent good fortune, they both played as though inspired, and the team from Whittle Crossing wondered what had hit them.

In a small town such as Daniel Creek, the people were as enthusiastic about their Junior as they were about their Senior Team. As a result, the match was watched with great interest by everyone in town.

It was not long before they realised that the local team had received a shot in the arm with the acquisition of Jet and Peter. Jet proved to be an almost unbeatable rover, and no mean goal kicker. Peter played in defence and was almost unbeatable.

Their outstanding play greatly impressed Harry Stewart and when he noticed Tom Blake, the coach from Whittle Crossing, edging towards the dressing-room of the local team as

the game was ending, he had no doubt about his intention.

He rose from the grandstand and moved towards the same place. There was no need for worry. Jack Williams had also noticed the move and was there before him, blocking the entrance to the dressing-room. He was addressing the coach.

"Looking for something, Tom?"

The coach laughed. "Got your watchdogs out, eh! I was just coming over to be ready to congratulate your team on its effort today."

"Very nice of you, I'm sure," said Harry Stewart, coming up from behind, "but you're wasting your time, Tom. The boys are staying in this area and belong to us."

The coach laughed. "Okay, fellows, but you can't blame me for trying. You've got a couple of champions in those two kids. Where did you dig them up from?"

"That's a trade secret, Tom."

"Who's looking after them?"

"Me," said Harry Stewart, decisively.

Tom Blake burst out laughing.

"I can see the cards are stacked against me, Harry. But treat them well, old boy, or we'll be ready to snap them up."

"I bet you will, you old buzzard," grinned Williams, "but Harry's personally interested in them, and you know what that means."

"It means they're two lucky lads," said Blake. "If ever you lose interest in the Daniel Creek Demons, Harry, you know where you'll be welcome."

"Thanks for the compliment, Tom. Now I'm sure you'll have enough to do looking after your battered heroes. I think the final siren is due to go any minute."

It was a very elated team which returned to its rooms at the end of the game. To begin the season with a six-goal win over Whittle Crossing was something they had never done before. There was no doubt in the minds of any of the players, or the coach, as to the source of their inspiration.

"Thanks, fellows," said Bill Langforth, the Daniel Creek coach. "Jet and Peter have put some backbone into the side. Don't forget now, midweek practice on Wednesday."

"I don't know if we'll be able to make that," said Peter. "We're both going out to Mr Stewart's station and that's almost 100 kilometres out."

"We'll sort that out for you, don't worry," said Langforth. "Now off you go and see if you can't get some pointers by watching the main game."

Mr and Mrs Stewart picked Jet and Peter up at their quarters at six o'clock, after helping celebrate a double victory for the town with

Mr and Mrs Williams in their private flat at the hotel. Both boys had their luggage out on the pavement waiting, though not before Mrs Williams had given them a final once-over.

"Can't have you going out from here not looking your best," she said. "May Stewart would wonder what had happened to me."

She need not have worried. Two tubbed and scrubbed boys, in their neat new clothing greeted Stewart and his wife when they eventually arrived.

An enormous Cadillac drew up at the curb. The boys were looking it over with interest when they suddenly caught sight of Harry Stewart behind the wheel. Jet's first impulse was to run for it. Peter grabbed him. He too was over-awed by such opulence, but determined to put on as bold a front as possible.

Mrs Stewart cast an appraising eye over them and apparently what she saw was satisfactory, for she smiled and called out, "You look even better than you did on the football field, boys. Harry will put your bags in the boot. Hop in."

They opened the door and slid on to the back seat, feeling a little red and embarrassed. Peter could see that Jet was as uneasy as he was himself, and wondered if in the end it might not be too much for the boy.

Mrs Stewart could sense their uneasiness. She was a little unsure, herself, how this might all work out, and how much personal responsibility she would need to take for the welfare of the boys.

Her husband appeared to be totally unaware that there could be any problems. He was so used to making things work out properly that he had no misgivings at all about this present venture.

A moment later the huge car glided off down the main street of the town. It was soon purring along at 100 kilometres an hour on the wide tarred road, which extended some distance from the town before it met the earth roads common to the whole area.

Peter and Jet lay back on the padded seat, with the armrest between them, feeling a little like royalty, and wondering when it was all going to end.

Night fell soon afterwards, but the powerful beams of the headlights lit up the road for a kilometre ahead. In addition to the normal lighting, the car was equipped with special spotlights. Mr Stewart now reduced his speed.

"We don't usually make this run at night," he explained over his shoulder. "There's too much wild life."

As he spoke, a large red kangaroo jumped across the road, 100 metres ahead. He jammed on the brakes.

"If you see one, there's often another," he

commented. As if to illustrate his point, another kangaroo jumped out across the road, a few metres ahead of the car.

"What happens if you hit one, Mr Stewart?" asked Peter.

"At the least a dent in your car which costs seventy or eighty dollars to get beaten out."

"That's if you're lucky," added Mrs Stewart. "Once we hit a 'roo that bounced off the bonnet and came through the windscreen."

"What did you do?"

"Stopped the car and got out in a hurry," was the reply. "We were all scratched and bruised but, strange to say, the 'roo was unhurt. After tearing up the upholstery a bit, it got out through a door and went on its way."

"What about emus?" asked Jet. "Do you have many round these parts?"

"Boy," said Mr Stewart, "you name it, we have it, from emus to wild goats."

About an hour after leaving the town, a great whitewashed pile of rocks, holding a wooden sign, YULLAMOOLOO PLAINS 32 KM, showed that they had come to the station turnoff.

In due course they passed over a strong, wide grid, that served as a cattle stop. It was flanked on either side by concrete posts, and ornamented with the whitewashed wheels of an old bullock drag.

As if to make sure that no one would be unaware that they were on the road to the station, across the top, high in the air, was another big piece of timber with the name of the station cut deeply into it. Peter and Jet were very impressed.

"This is where you begin to earn your keep," said Stewart to the boys.

"Despite all modern progress we still have gates in this place. We've often promised ourselves that one day we'll put grids in this section to keep the cattle in, but somehow we've never got round to it."

"How many gates have you got?" asked Peter.

"Twenty on this section, but as we have a couple of hundred paddocks, you can see that we have a few hundred gates."

They were not left long in doubt as to what Stewart meant about earning their keep. For the next hour Jet and Peter hopped in and out, at regular intervals, undoing gates, letting the car through, doing them up again, and then climbing back into the car. Though he did not know it, Peter was learning one of the first lessons of the country—one never left a gate open. Gates, like the flies, the goats, the wild donkeys, the emus, and the kangaroos, not to mention a camel or two, were an accepted part of the country.

Just the same, he found it astonishing that on the main track from the road to the station, the gates should be of such a variety and, in some cases, so difficult to open and close.

Harry Stewart patiently bore the fumblings while pretending not to hear his muffled exclamations as a more obstinate piece of wire refused to loop back over a post. Occasionally, in an incautious moment, Peter released some weird contraption, consisting of a large stick attached to some fencing wire stretched between two posts, only to have the whole paraphernalia suddenly either hit him a smart blow on the hand or nearly take his head off.

Some twenty kilometres along the track, they reached an area which appeared to be well covered with vegetation and trees.

"We're on the Yullamooloo River flats," Stewart told them. "It has a flood plain, nearly ten kilometres wide on each side, and so we've a magnificent stretch of country. The station itself is built on high ground out of the reach of the floods—a very wise precaution, as you'll see next flood time."

As he spoke, they began the descent to the river, and the boys saw the massive concrete low-level crossing. On one side the river was dammed up, and they could make out a sheet of water, but in the darkness they could not see how far it stretched. The car soon roared over the smooth surface of the crossing and up the other side.

Four gates later, Stewart announced, "That's the last one, fellows. We're in the home paddock."

Shortly afterwards the road began to climb. Peter's ears popped and he knew they had gained some altitude. The road was wide and well graded and he could not see anything except the rough walls of the hill, where the ground had been cut away to allow the road to pass through. Then they appeared to come on to a long, wide plateau and ahead they could see a blaze of lights.

"Home," said Mrs Stewart. "It's always a welcome sight after the long journey from town."

"You will insist on going there by car," said Mr Stewart. "I could fly you out in about a quarter of the time by plane."

"Plane?" asked Peter. "You have an aeroplane here?"

"Yes, two. You'll see."

By now they had driven into a wide, open space, floodlit by several powerful lights. There seemed to be buildings in all directions. As they came to a stop, about half a dozen dogs came running towards them, barking and making a great fuss.

Another half a dozen came from the other direction and, as the boys got out of the car, they seemed to be surrounded by a mass of fighting dogs. Mr Stewart gave a loud roar and the dogs ran in all directions.

"We have a team of Aborigines up to help for the time being," he said, "and our dogs and their dogs are always fighting each other. They know their own territory, but every now and again one lot or the other crosses it. Just yell at them. They'll stop."

He took out the boys' luggage from the boot.

"You can use a room in the quarters at the house until we get you set up," he told them. "We all eat together in the kitchen—the boys, my manager, and the others. Mrs Stewart and I used to have a separate dining-room when we had the kids, but we'd be too lonely using it on our own now. In any case we'd look too stuck-up eating alone. We all have to work together here, and so I don't see why we shouldn't eat together."

They moved over to the homestead. It was built high off the ground and was surrounded by tall trees and rich shrubbery.

As they passed through the doors, Peter noticed the thickness of the walls and the height of the ceiling. All the rooms appeared enormous and both boys paused for a moment at the sight of the furnishings.

Harry Stewart grinned.

"Looks like something out of the last century, doesn't it fellows? It is too. When we took over this place, it was filled with what we thought was a lot of old junk, but when we examined it more closely, we found we had a treasure-house of antique furniture. We had a chap up here for a month or two restoring it. This place is now marked by the National Trust to be preserved as a historical monument."

"Heck," said Peter, "it's like a museum."

Mrs Stewart laughed, "And Harry and I are two of the old fossils in it, eh?"

"I'm sorry, Mrs Stewart. I didn't mean to be rude, but I've never seen all this sort of ju—, uh furniture except in a museum."

"You'll get used to it, laddie, and possibly enjoy it as much as we do."

Much to the boys' relief, the room into which they were finally ushered was furnished in a more modern manner.

"I'm glad this room hasn't got any old furniture," said Peter. "That sort of stuff is worth thousands of dollars. I'd be frightened to use anything in case I broke it."

"Me too," agreed Jet, who was thoroughly overawed, "but I can't understand why when something gets older, it gets more valuable."

They unpacked their soap and towels and, finding a bathroom nearby, had a quick wash.

A full tea was set out for them, and when they had eaten enough, Mr Stewart suggested that they go to bed.

"We don't do much on Sundays, and so I'll introduce you to my boys tomorrow, and they can show you around," he said. "Sleep well."

"We'll do that all right, sir," said Peter.

Stewart looked at him.

"For goodness sake, son, don't call me 'sir' in front of the others. They'd laugh their heads off. Round here they officially call me 'Boss,' and unofficially, quite a number of other names which you will doubtless learn in due course."

Two very excited boys slept very soundly that night.

Just before dropping off to sleep Peter muttered to himself, "It just can't be true."

Chapter Three

PLENTY OF OPENING FOR ERROR

PETER ROSE AND DRESSED quietly as soon as it was light. Jet lay snoring in his bed, but Peter did not disturb him. The boy was anxious to see by daylight the vast areas he had passed through in the darkness of the night before.

Their room opened on to one of the wide verandahs which surrounded the house. Peter found that he was looking out from the homestead, over the wide plateau, to the rugged grandeur of the country below.

He was not one to try to analyse his feelings very deeply, and yet, as he looked, he was conscious of an intense feeling of wonder and delight. Perhaps it was this same feeling that had inspired an early pioneer to found Yullamooloo station, and to build his home on this section overlooking it all.

Straight ahead the plains ran as far as the eye could see. On either side were rugged ranges, whose steep cliffs presented a variety of colours in areas where they had weathered away over the ages. In the distance, with the rising of the sun, he could see that the hills had become an indistinct purple. They provided a worthy backdrop to a scene of such magnificent beauty.

He could see the river-course marked by the line of tall white trees which lined its banks. A little closer, a tributary seemed to skirt the hill on which the homestead stood.

As he moved from the verandah, Peter could see that the main house was surrounded by workshops. Some distance away were a number of cottages and a bungalow.

There was no movement except at the machine shed, where a tall, thin young man was tinkering with the engine of a huge transporter.

Peter walked over. The young man appeared not to notice him, but in a moment a voice from the depths of the vehicle said, "Hand me a shifting spanner."

Peter did so.

"Thanks."

There was silence for a moment.

"You must be the new kid."

"Yes."

"Hand me a small screwdriver."

Peter did so.

"Thanks."

This went on for a few minutes, until at last a head emerged from the truck, and Peter saw a

long, thin face staring quizzically at him.

"Well," said Peter, for the sake of something to say.

The young man put out a hand covered with grease and oil. "I'm Tim Stewart," he said.

Peter took the hand and said, "I'm Peter Devlin."

His hand was now covered with oil and grime, and he felt uncomfortable about it.

Tim Stewart burst out laughing.

"Dad said you were a polite sort of cove, but I didn't think you'd be that polite." He threw Peter a piece of rag. "Here, wipe your paw."

"Thank you, Mr Stewart."

"Who? Round here they all call me Tim. That includes you. Pass me those pliers, please."

At that moment Harry Stewart came in.

"Ah. I see you've met Tim. You'll get to know him in time. He's a nut-case you know. We call him the Mad Inventor round here. He invents things which never work."

Tim looked at his father with a look of mock pain on his face.

"Father, one of these days you'll be sorry for those words."

"Not half as sorry as I am when one of your crackpot inventions wrecks the place," said Mr Stewart.

He pointed to a large area, which was closed off from the rest of the workshop.

"See that place, Peter. You enter it at the risk of your life. You never can tell what young Tim's going to be up to next. Whatever it is, I can assure you it will be dangerous."

"Come, dad. You haven't seen the latest—my pneumatic door-shutter. Works on compressed air."

"Tell me where you have installed it and I'll keep well clear of the place."

"Over at my quarters," said Tim.

"Good. That gives me an excuse for not going over. I want you to take young Peter here and his mate, Jet. They can share your bungalow. You and Les have plenty of room and I think the four of you will all get on well together."

"Les and I had already decided on that last night, dad. We want a couple of willing lads to keep the place clean, make our beds, do some cooking, and a few other things round the place."

"They'll do what they have to, I'm sure, but they're not here to be housekeepers to clean up your mess."

Tim gave a great sigh of disappointment. It was apparent to Peter that he had assumed the role of the local funny man, but just the same Peter was beginning to like him. He was probably not more than four or five years older than Peter in any case.

"Tim and Les live by themselves," explained Mr Stewart, pointing to one of the larger buildings. "We couldn't stand them in the house any longer, and so we booted them out."

"Some parents," interrupted Tim, "not mentioning any names, mind you, are so hard to live with that their children leave them."

"Okay, fellow. Enough of the backchat. You can take the boys over to your place after breakfast."

Then he turned to Peter. "Come on, son, we'll give you some breakfast and then you can go over to your quarters. You'll get used to Tim in time. Anyway, Les is more sensible."

When they were out of earshot Stewart said, "He's a fine kid, Peter, and pretty brainy in fact. He and his brother really run this place. They live away from us so that they can be independent, but they come over for meals during the day or when they feel like it. You'll enjoy living over there with them. Never a dull moment. Les is rather more serious, but you'll need to watch him too. He likes his little joke with the rest."

"What will you want us to do, Mr Stewart?"

"Everything, son. On a station you have to be jack-of-all-trades — mechanic, carpenter, plumber, electrician, vet. You must be prepared to work till you drop some days, and then rest some time when things are slack.

There are jobs that can't wait. If a mill breaks down, we fix it; if a vehicle cracks up, we repair it; if a fence is torn down, we put it back up again; if an animal gets sick, we treat it. There is no 'tomorrow' in this country."

Peter returned to his room and wakened Jet by dragging him out of his bed on to the floor. For a moment the boy appeared to want to make a fight of it.

"Relax, Jet. You take things too seriously. A little horsing round between friends never did anyone any harm."

"Well, don't try your luck too far," said Jet.

Peter did not reply. Jet had a long way to go before he would lose his suspicion of the world. They washed hurriedly and then made their way to the kitchen.

After breakfast Tim appeared.

"Want something to eat?" asked his father.

"No thanks. Les cooked a slashing breakfast—a pound of bacon and eight eggs between us."

"Good heavens, you'll have the fowls working overtime just keeping you two supplied."

"Les and I are working men and we need much more to keep us going than you idle rich, living here at the homestead, father."

"Under those circumstances then, son, I'm sure you will have enough energy to go out and fix the mill in Allunga—it's only twenty-five kilometres."

"Me and my big mouth," muttered Tim. "Okay, the job's as good as done, Dad."

"It had better be. Now take the kids over to your place. They can give you a hand."

As they took their gear over to the bungalow, Jet looked round.

"Can't see any shearing sheds," he said.

"No, you wouldn't want to have to drive the sheep up here. See." Tim pointed.

Below them on the plateau there was another large group of buildings.

"We've got the shearers' quarters down there. It's a survival from the old days when the squatters and the men kept apart. They still do to a certain extent. When the men are on the job in the shed, we go down there only on their invitation."

"Where do our mob live—do you have any Aborigines?" asked Jet.

"They come out and work like the rest. We've tried to make their quarters a bit better, but they don't like anything too classy."

"Our mob never had anything too classy in any case," said Jet, "so I don't suppose they'd know."

"You do," said Tim, rather directly. "If you didn't, you wouldn't be asked to live with us."

"I can always go down below and live," put in Jet, equally directly.

"Now you're getting upperty—racial discrimination and all that sort of thing," said Tim. "I resent the fact that you don't think I'm good enough to live with. I'll have you know that in this place I even consider myself equal to you. Now let's cut out the idiot stuff, Jet. We're living and working together and that's the end of it. Come on, I'll show you my very latest invention, the pneumatic door-opener."

By now the three of them had crossed over to the bungalow and were standing on the verandah.

"See," said Tim, indicating a button on the wall near the door, "I press this, and hey presto!"

Nothing happened, but from somewhere there came the hiss of escaping air.

"Blast!" said Tim. "She's sprung a leak." He turned the door handle, but the door refused to budge.

"Blast again! She's stuck. Nip through the window, Peter, and undo the lock inside, will you? There's a little piston that pushes the lock open, and then the door gently swings open too."

Peter put down his luggage and slipped through the window. He turned the handle of the lock from the inside. The moment the door was released it swung back with such force that it flung him across the room, where he landed with a crash against the opposite wall.

Tim, seeing the door open, began to come through, but it had not finished its mad capers. With equal force it slammed shut, throwing Tim right off the verandah past the astonished Jet.

At the same moment a violent explosion blew off part of the roof, and shook the house like an earthquake.

Peter had just got to his feet when he was flung down again. As he picked himself up for the second time in order to make a quick exit through the rear door, he found that he was contesting the narrow space with another young man, still in his pyjamas, who was also making his exit with great speed.

They sprawled together on the floor, as a shower of plaster descended on them. Then, in a more orderly fashion, but with no less speed, they ran through the house and out through the back door.

There the young man, who Peter assumed must be Les, stood for a moment regarding the shattered roof and the large cloud of dust now just settling.

Pausing only to yell loudly, "I'll kill him!

I'll kill the silly cow!" he ran round to the front of the house.

Tim was just picking himself up. Jet was a hundred metres away and still running.

"Something must have gone wrong," said the shaken Tim.

Chapter Four

MEET LES STEWART

Mr stewart had just started a truck to go down to the shearing sheds, when he heard the terrific blast from the bungalow. He spun the wheel and raced over, arriving just in time to prevent an enraged Les from giving full vent to his feelings in a personal assault on his brother.

"He nearly killed me," yelled Les.

"My beautiful invention has gone up the spout," wailed Tim.

"Shut up," shouted Harry Stewart. "I seem to have a couple of maniacs on my hands. What happened?"

"It was the door, sir," said Peter, trying to explain.

"Don't call me 'sir'," yelled Stewart. "I told you that before. Now, what happened?"

"Ruddy house blew up; that's what happened," said Jet, who had now returned. "Frightened the ruddy stuffing out of me."

"He ought to be in a nut-house," said Les.

"There I am in my bedroom, about to get dressed, and next minute—wham—I'm blown out of the house."

"Let's go inside and see what damage he's done," said the practical Harry Stewart, but though they pounded, kicked, and threw themselves against the front door, it once again refused to open.

Stewart strode round the house, followed by Tim and Peter, while Jet hovered well in the background. Les crawled back into his room through a window.

The main living-room was a wreck. Peter could see that had he not been flung across the room by the door he would have received the full force of the explosion. As they entered, the remains of a forty-gallon drum fell from the ceiling on to the floor with a great thump. It missed Mr Stewart by a whisker.

"Great jumping Jonah!" he yelled. "Where the blazes did that come from?"

"It was my air-reservoir," said Tim. "Appears to have burst."

"It's nothing to what I'll do to you, if you ever do this again."

"He won't," said Les, reappearing from his room, and now fully clothed. "Next time it will be something else."

"You'd better rouse old Larry up and get him to help you repair the roof," said Mr

Stewart, "and the door too. It's jammed shut."

He turned to Peter. "I don't know if it's safe leaving you over here."

"I think I'll take a chance," was the reply. "Tim can't invent something new every day, so we ought to be safe in between times."

"Thanks," said Tim, "I'll remember that."

"What about you?" asked Stewart, turning to Jet who had now entered the house.

"Dunno," said Jet. "Might be safer living over in the explosives store."

"I'll remember that too," said Tim. "Nobody has any time for a genius."

"It's unanimous, at least," said Les. "Come on, kids. I'll show you your rooms—that is, if there's anything left of them."

Fortunately the rear of the house was undamaged, apart from the loss of some plaster from the walls. Two rooms were ready for them.

Peter immediately began to unpack. For the first time for a year, he had a place of his own with all the things he was used to—neat furniture, a wardrobe, a small dressing-table, and even a writing-desk.

Jet stood in the middle of his room, gazing about him. He was at a loss. The room reminded him of his city days and of his foster-mother. He blinked back the tears, and reminded himself that he did not fit into this sort of thing.

He was torn between the remembrance of the kindly attention of the late Mrs Haynes, and the less organised and free existence with his father, Jacky Windmill. He was unable to decide what he wanted.

Here lay a future, he knew, that was much better than anything he had expected. What could he hope for if he stayed with "his mob," as he still preferred to think of them? Was his friendship with Peter too high a price to pay for the loss of his former freedom, even if he did not know what future that freedom offered him?

Standing in the room he knew he was facing a decision.

"Take what you can get, son," his father had always said. "If the other mob offer it to you, take it. They owe us something."

He remembered the last brief interview with his father, when he had decided to cast in his lot with Peter. Jacky Windmill had been almost eager that he should go.

"Okay," he thought, coming to a decision, "I'll stick around and see what happens."

He flung his case under the bed, but did not open it or put his clothes away in the drawers.

Les Stewart was calling both of them. Jet moved outside and found that the young man was standing near a truck laden with all sorts of gear.

"I've got to go out and fix that windmill, while Tim repairs the house. You two had better come. You'll get to know a bit of the country." Les noticed they were still in their good clothing.

"Get some old stuff on, fellows—shorts and a shirt. We may get a bit dirty."

They returned a few minutes later and the truck roared away. Of Tim there was no sign. He was probably still trying to work out what had happened to his brainchild.

Les was also tall and slim, and about three of four years older than his brother. He appeared to be a clear-cut and decisive type of chap. Both boys felt he was the sort of fellow it would be wise not to cross.

Just the same, Les was friendly enough. As they left the plateau and drove down to the plain country, he was quick to point out anything of interest.

They crossed the home paddock and ran along a well-constructed airstrip. A large building at one end apparently held the planes, but they did not go near enough for the boys to see them.

"What sort of planes do you have?" Peter asked.

"Cessnas. We've got a 177 which we use for the station work, and dad uses the larger one —a Golden Eagle—for business trips, for flying interstate, or for going to other properties, It's pretty fast."

"Who's the pilot?"

"We all have our certificates, but I do most of the flying, particularly on the station. Dad isn't too keen on the smaller plane, but I think she's a beauty. You'll see her in action in due course."

"Do you always use planes for getting around?"

"Of course, and trucks and motor bikes."

"Have you any horses?"

"What for?"

"Rounding up and things."

"Peter boy, you've a lot to learn. Even if we had any horses here, I don't know what we would use them for now. We used to have a few years ago, but in the end there was no work for them to do."

"But what about boundary riding and all that sort of thing?"

"Peter lad, you've been reading too much Banjo Paterson. That was long ago. Now we do it all by plane. You'll see."

As they talked, they were moving at a fast pace along a well-graded road, stopping now and again to pass through the ubiquitous gates, which had to be opened and closed.

"I heard that you have 200 paddocks. How do you know where you are?"

"Every paddock has a name. We use all native names here—native to the country, I mean, and originally Aboriginal. I think the chap who opened the place up must have had a dictionary, as 200 Aboriginal names take a lot of thinking up! We've a master plan of the property at the homestead and another at our place. One day you can look at it and find your way about. Of course as well as the paddocks there are vast areas that are unfenced.

"These roads," said Jet. "Who made them?"

"We have a chap working full-time with a grader. The better the roads, the quicker we get from place to place. It pays us to keep them in good condition. Even so, sometimes in the winter the roads get in a mess and have to be redone. So one way and another, old John Angus has a full-time job. We give him a hand now and again."

They were out at the windmill in three-quarters of an hour. Peter looked for the familiar tank and troughs, but there weren't any troughs and certainly no tank.

Instead a large concrete basin had been constructed and this was supplied with water directly from the windmill.

"What's the idea?" Peter asked.

"Serves two purposes. It lets the sheep and cattle get to plenty of water easily, and also, if the water level is down, it can be seen from the air—makes it much easier to tell if a pump isn't working."

They unloaded the heavy gear from the back of the truck while Les examined the windmill.

"We're lucky," he remarked. "A pin has sheared off the pump-rod. We may have to fish round a bit to get the rod up but that won't take long. What I don't like is having to put in new washers. Nowadays the stuff they send us is so poor that it just doesn't last. Plastic isn't much good. Give me the good old leather washers any time."

There were large flocks of merino sheep near the dam and, even though the boys were working quite noisily, quite a number of red kangaroos hopped by quite close to them.

The repairs were completed in an hour or two and, after reloading the truck, they set off back to the homestead.

It was a bright, though not hot, day and Les was looking forward to an afternoon at the swimming pool. It was this perhaps that caused him to drive faster than usual. In the middle of the day, the last thing he expected was to have to avoid a kangaroo on the road.

The speed was unfortunate for them and the kangaroo—an animal which should have been browsing in the shade of a tree at that hour, instead of actively courting death by crossing the road.

It might have reached the other side safely were it not for the fact that there was a fence lining the road there, so that, as the animal reached the other side, it cannoned off the fence back into the path of the speeding truck.

Les instinctively swung to the left, knocking down a long length of fence, before managing to pull up. They were all jolted and shaken, but not otherwise hurt, and because there was no other way, they slid out by the driver's door and surveyed the damage.

The wire fence had been torn down for fully fifty metres and most of this was now wound round the wheels, steering rods, and drive shaft of the truck. Of the 'roo there was no sign.

Les examined the situation, scratching his head. "By heck, if they hear of this at the station, I'll never live it down," he remarked. "Grandma's knitting has nothing on this stuff—and a lot of it is barbed wire too."

"What are we going to do?"

"Cut it off, if we can. I don't think the truck is unduly damaged, but it's going to take hours to get this off."

"Let's begin," said Jet. "Don't know who's the worse, you or your brother. You sure do a bit of damage in one day."

Peter grinned, but said nothing. Instead he found some hacksaws among the tools. He handed one to Jet and they began the laborious task of cutting the wire away from the rear wheels.

Les took a pair of wire cutters and started snipping away at the front. When the truck was nearly free, he left the boys to work alone, and trudged off with an axe, to cut down some small trees to replace the fence posts. It was fortunate for the truck that in this stretch all the fence posts had been made of wood which was fairly old, and this had splintered away without adding too much damage to the vehicle.

The rest of the wire came free eventually and Jet picked it up and threw it well away from the road. Fortunately the truck was carrying the usual coil of wire on it for use in case of breaks in the fences. They strung this along the new fence posts that Les had prepared.

It was late afternoon before they had finished. The truck motor seemed to go just as well as before, and the stretch of new fence was not very conspicuous.

Jet found a dead sheep nearby and dragged it over to the fence. He let the barbed wire tear off some of the wool, so that it hung in natural strands on the wire. He dragged another dead sheep alongside the fence and wiped the ground clear of tyre marks with some branches.

Les watched all this with astonishment.

"What do you think you're doing?" he asked.

Jet grinned. "My last boss was an expert at cutting down fences," he explained, "and I'm an expert at putting them back original like."

Les threw his head back and laughed. "Seems that we could go into the sheep-stealing business in a big way, with you to help us, Jet."

They climbed back into the truck, but this time proceeded with greater caution.

"Look, fellows," said Les, as they drew near to the homestead, "don't mention this little mishap to the others. Okay?"

"What's it worth?" said the practical Jet.

"A good clip over the ear if you do," said Les, "and all the dirty jobs round the place for a week."

"All right," said Jet, "no offence meant. I was just asking."

"We wouldn't tell on you, Les," said Peter mischievously. "One goat in the family is about all your pa and ma could stand."

"Thanks," said Les. "Whatever your motive, I'll appreciate your shutting up about it. You won't lose."

The incident with the fence was a very trivial one, but it had the effect of bringing the two boys and Les together in a common understanding.

Tim could make his mistakes and be the

local buffoon without loss of face, but Peter became aware, right from that time, that Les could be very sensitive in matters which reflected on his own abilities and skills.

At the end of the first day Peter felt that he had already learnt much. It was apparent that there would be no lack of happenings in life at Yullamooloo.

Chapter Five

THE WOOL-BALE LOADER

IN THE NEXT FEW DAYS the boys were taken in hand by Tim who, now that the house was repaired and the door unstuck, had completely forgotten the episode and was now planning some equally dangerous new invention.

They found him, however, a very practical mechanic. He took them to part of the large machine shed, where there were about a dozen motor bikes. The shed was as clean as a new pin and it was evident that each bike had been fully serviced and was kept ready to use at any time.

"It's a big job just keeping these machines serviceable," Tim explained. "In the shearing season we have a full-time mechanic, but in between times we do the work ourselves. You'll notice that they're all trailbikes with plenty of ground clearance. They take a lot of hammering, as the Aboriginal stockmen have to keep moving on them at shearing time, rounding up 40 000 sheep."

"Finding the strays must be like looking for a needle in a haystack," said Peter, thinking of his own past experiences with Jet when they did the same thing on horseback.

"No, not the way we do it. Each bike is equipped with a walkie-talkie radio, and usually Les and I take it in turns spotting the sheep from the air, and driving them towards the waiting men."

He pointed to the machines.

"You will notice that they all have those squares of board on the tank and on the pillion. That's for the sheep dogs. Two go out on each bike."

"This I must see," said Peter. "It's quite different from what we've done."

"We'll be doing a bit of rounding up over the next few months—moving sheep from one paddock to another and so on. You'll get plenty of action."

It was obvious that before that happened the boys must learn about the mechanics of the bikes and how to ride them.

They pored over the manuals and instruction books, and whenever one of the bikes was pulled down, Tim found he had two eager helpers.

He was a good instructor, and taught the boys all about the mechanics of the bikes before they rode them. He put two bikes on their stands, and taught the boys how to kick the engines over and use all the gears before he allowed them to take the bikes out.

Then the great day arrived. Loading two bikes on the truck, he took Peter and Jet to a fairly clear area to give them their first ride.

Peter was no different from any other boy of his age in regard to riding a motor bike. He imagined himself a natural speedway champion, capable of instant control over his mount. Jet, on the other hand, was prepared to meet things as they came.

When Peter had a spill, and he had many, he regarded the situation as a conflict between him and the bike, in which he must emerge the winner at all costs. Jet regarded his mishaps as part of the learning process, and simply picked himself up and got on again.

As a result, it was Jet who became the better rider, and he could do things on his bike that only brought Peter to disaster. Peter resented this and tried too hard, with the result that he continued to suffer many startling spills.

Tim watched it all good-naturedly. "Never mind, Pete," he commented. "You'll do all right in time. Jet will probably make the better rider, but he'll walk home more often than you, when his machine conks out."

To Peter's satisfaction Jet had one major mishap, although it was not really his own

fault, when his throttle jammed. In the confusion, the boy allowed the machine to continue along at its mad pace, without trying at least to kick it out of gear.

Tim raced after him, shouting instructions, but the bike kept on, and stopped only when it came to a sudden dip and ploughed halfway across a large pool, leaving Jet sitting up to his waist in water, still hanging on tightly to the machine.

Peter came up soon afterwards to help the bedraggled boy pull the ruined bike from the pool. They loaded the broken-down machine on the truck and returned to the shed. The three of them then spent the rest of the afternoon pulling it completely down and drying it out. If nothing else, they learned considerably more about the workings of the engine.

Jet was not at all upset by the mishap, nor greatly concerned about the possible damage to the bike. Peter, on the other hand, was glad it had not happened to him, as he would have worried about the effects of the water on the motor.

Tim's only comment was, "Good thing you were using the old machines. I don't think Les would have liked Jet's turning it into a submarine."

Tim left them to complete the job of reassembling the bike, after he had made sure that they knew what to do. He retired to the deepest recesses of his workshop, to work on a contrivance which, he assured the boys, would cut down the work of loading the wool truck by half.

Wisely, neither boy tried to find out the mysteries of this next contribution to the welfare of mankind, but remembered Mr Stewart's advice and kept well away.

There was no doubt that Tim had a fixation in regard to using compressed air in all his contrivances.

"There's only one thing that's free in this world," he had informed the boys, "and that's air. Used the right way, it can perform miracles."

In the middle of the week, Les took a vehicle into Daniel Creek early in the afternoon. Peter and Jet accompanied him and he released them in the town to go to their football training. Les was a squash player, and apparently made it a practice, when making the midweek trip into town for stores, mail, and other items, to plan for his recreation as well.

This suited the boys very well. They were itching to get into regular team practice. Mr Stewart had supplied them with a few old footballs, which they used in every spare minute on the station.

Jet was seldom seen in his spare time doing

anything else but kicking, bouncing, or in some way working with a football. One thing he and Peter were able to work together well on was passing, and they practised after tea each night until they were exhausted.

The result was, however, that in due time they became so expert that, no matter where Peter suddenly punched the ball, Jet was there, in a flash, to collect it and run on.

Though they did not yet know it, they were becoming a very formidable combination. Harry Stewart watched them from afar, but did not interfere except, now and again, in an offhand way, to proffer some advice, which he was pleased to notice they always followed, sometimes with good effect, sometimes with no effect at all.

Harry had a wise old head and did not press too hard.

"After all, they're only kids," he said to his wife, one day. "We'll let them develop one ability at a time, and at the same time see that they don't get into bad habits."

Just the same, it did his heart good to hear the steady sound of football boots hitting leather. His own family had taken up other sports, Les squash and tennis, his girls swimming, and Tim rugby.

Peter now felt on top of the world. People were interested in what he did, his future seemed assured, and he had the opportunity to take part in activities which he enjoyed and understood.

Joining boys of his own age in the football team was also a great boost. Not that Bill Langforth gave them much time to talk.

"You're either on the field to work, or you're on the other side of the pickets," he warned them. "You don't win football matches by fooling around at practice."

Just the same, firm friendships were built up between the team members and Peter and Jet, both from personal regard and also because of the obvious ability of both boys. Many of the team were preparing for their final school examinations. This reminded Peter of his own determination to continue his studies. When they had finished their workouts and were waiting for Les, Peter and Jet moved over to see Mr Williams and to ask for the use of some notepaper to write to the local school. They not only obtained the notepaper, but also a very delicious tea, and Jack Williams promised to see the principal of the school himself. When Les picked them up, he was surprised when they turned down his offer of a meal at a café, but judged from the satisfied look on both their faces that they had already fared well.

Next morning Tim told Peter and Jet to come out early to assist him in rigging up his most recent gadget for making work lighter for those at Yullamooloo.

"I can't claim it's original," he commented, as the boys carried the various pieces of the machine over to the shearing shed. "We've one for loading bags on to the truck; it works on a spring and raises bags or bales of hay on to the tray. It can be operated by one man. This machine does the same thing for the wool bales, but it's worked, of course, by compressed air."

Both boys were taken aback, but Tim reassured them, "Don't worry about this one. Nothing can go wrong with it; it's foolproof."

"So was the door," said Peter, "and look what happened."

"This is different," said Tim, as he bolted the lifting mechanism into place. "It can be adjusted to take any weight and to work as slowly as you want."

The assembled loader looked simple enough, and there appeared little that could go wrong with it. The bale was loaded on to a type of fork, a small lever was pulled gently, and the bale rose to the desired height. Extension frames could be added to raise the height as each layer was complete.

"When the bale reaches its correct height," Tim explained, "a cam-wheel tips the fork down at an angle so that the bale slides off just where we want it. The beauty is that one man can load a whole transport."

He connected up the air bottles. The lifting fork was on the ground and they manhandled a bale on to it. Tim gave the lever a small turn and slowly the wool bale rose, was tipped over and slid into its appointed place.

For some reason, however, the lifting fork, after regaining the horizontal, failed to drop to the ground.

"We may have to ride it down," said Tim. "Jet, you go up and stand on it."

Jet did so, very reluctantly, but the lifting fork came down as required, and he stepped off on to the ground. They manhandled a second bale on to the machine. It too slid into its required place, but again the fork refused to drop.

Peter jumped up on the fork and rode it down. Unfortunately, at that moment the affair decided to do things its own way, and before Peter could jump off, the fork rose again with such speed that Peter was catapulted on to the roof of the shed.

He landed with a resounding crash, rolled down the incline, managed to grab the guttering and dropped with a thud on to Tim who was immediately below him.

Neither of them was hurt, but there was great confusion before they sorted themselves out.

"That's the last time I'm going to have anything to do with your inventions," said Peter. "One day someone is going to get hurt."

"Come on, fellows," begged Tim, who had now risen and dusted himself down. "Don't leave me now. It's only a minor adjustment. Just help me put the bales on. I'll ride the fork down."

There was no need. By some perverse chance the fork had returned to the ground. They loaded a bale. Tim touched the lever. The machine did all it was designed to do, and did it perfectly.

"I think I've got it!" shouted Tim.

They decided to call Mr Stewart over to see the masterpiece.

Peter walked over to one of the sheds where the man was working. "Tim's automatic wool-bale loader is working perfectly, Mr Stewart, and he'd like you to come over and see it."

"Impossible," said Mr Stewart. "Nothing he makes ever works perfectly."

"It is now," said Peter. "It threw me on the roof about fifteen minutes ago but I think it's safe now."

"It'd better be," said Mr Stewart, starting to walk over to the scene of activity.

They were about twenty metres away when once again the machine decided to take over. Instead of dropping the bale into place, it flung the bale into the air so that it came hurtling towards Peter and Mr Stewart at great speed.

A 150-kilogram bale of wool flying through the air is a force not to be argued with. Peter ran one way; Mr Stewart the other. The bale hit the ground between them and burst, its compressed contents spreading themselves over the fleeing pair.

Mr Stewart had so much wool over him that he would have been worth ten dollars at shearing time, with Peter bringing perhaps a little less.

There was nothing sheeplike in Stewart's roar of rage, however. He shook his fist at Tim who, seeing the damage he had caused, was departing for parts far away.

Jet was standing by, not sure as to whether he should take off too or stay and face the music.

Peter tried to calm the station owner.

"Don't be too hard on him, Mr Stewart. The thing really works. I think that perhaps a bit of dirt might have caused the valves to stick, and given an unequal pressure or allowed the pressure to build up too much. If Tim added a pressure gauge and filter in the system, and perhaps a safety. valve between the compressed air and the machine, I reckon most of his inventions would work."

Peter's words had the effect of quietening down old Mr Stewart.

"You may have something there, son," he said, looking over the loading gadget. "I hope you have. For once Tim has made something that could be really useful round here. He won't come back while I'm here, so I'd better go. Tell him what you think."

When Tim noticed the coast was clear, he came back. Peter expounded his idea.

"Hadn't thought of that," the young man replied. "We'll give it a go."

They unscrewed the air cylinder and took it back to the work shop.

This time, Tim attached a water trap, so that nothing but clean air entered the system.

The matter of fixing a pressure gauge and safety valve on the pipeline was also soon attended to. In due course they again re-assembled the machine and, watching the gauge for sudden fluctuations, began loading again. Everything went without a hitch.

"You've got a few brains in that head of yours," said Tim. "Go and ask dad to come over now."

To be on the safe side Mr Stewart and Peter approached the area obliquely, but this time there was no need for caution. The machine was operating at full speed in the manner for which it was designed.

After watching twenty to thirty bales go up without mishap, even Mr Stewart was impressed.

"It looks as if he's got a winner at last—cheap enough at the price I suppose, the price of one boy being hurled on the roof and a bale full of wool being strewn round the countryside. It's his cheapest invention to date—and what's more, it works for a change."

Chapter Six

STATIONS ARE NOT WHAT THEY USED TO BE

WHAT WAS CONSIDERED ROUTINE at Yullamooloo had a sense of adventure for Peter and was a new experience for Jet.

Les approached them one morning and took them both down to the hangar at the end of the airstrip.

"Ever been up in one of these?" he asked, as they moved over to the smaller plane.

"Not in one so small," said Peter. "I've been interstate in a jet."

"Right," said Les, "you're going to have to get used to this one. Find yourselves a tin each."

"What for?" asked Jet.

"You may need it. Until you get used to them, these small planes are rather inclined to upset you. Sometimes the ride is very bumpy and as we have to do a lot of turning you may feel a bit green."

"Thanks for the happy introduction," said Peter. "I reckon I'll be okay."

They helped Les push the plane out of the hangar on to a piece of tarred apron in front.

The plane was a Cessna 177 Cardinal. The boys were agog to learn details of it as Les tested the tyres and they helped him pump them up.

"Nothing much to tell," said Les. "She's capable of staying in the air for six hours at about 210 km/h. She's not pressurised, and so we don't take her up too high. We do most of our work pretty close to the ground."

Peter peered inside at the controls and the mass of instruments, and was very impressed.

"We're going to do a boundary run today," Les told them. "In the old days this used to take a whole team of men weeks to do. Now we do it in a few hours. You two get in the back seat. I want you to spot for me. Watch the fences for breaks, and when we cross over the windmills, make sure they're working."

Les warmed up the engine and taxied slowly on to the runway. The plane accelerated, and they were airborne before the boys realised it.

Though it was still early in the morning, the plane moved up and down as it rode the thermal currents in certain areas, but Peter did not feel as troubled by this as he was when Les took the machine into a sharp turn to inspect a windmill.

Peter's instinct was to pull against his safety

straps and he felt nauseated until Les called out, "Let yourself go with the plane." He found this helped, and he began to take more interest in what was going on below. Jet appeared to be taking this new experience in his stride.

From the air they could see the vast paddocks stretching in all directions, with the great road system running through them all. Despite the large number of paddocks, Les seemed to know where he was at all times, naming the paddocks as they flew over them.

He was apparently making an assessment of the number of sheep in each paddock, for now and again he dipped the nose of the plane and turned on a siren. Sheep, which had been under trees or not in view, immediately began to move.

"Don't want to disturb them too much," Les yelled back over his shoulder, "but as you can see, this is how we spot them and get them moving at shearing time."

They disturbed a large herd of goats.

"Bet they're a nuisance," yelled Peter.

"They can be, but recently we've been rounding them up and sending them south. There's quite an export market for their meat at times to the Near North countries. We try to keep them moving so they won't denude the countryside, but they break the fences down. If they get too bad we have to get shooters in."

By now Peter was getting used to the plane and had found the fresh-air vent in the roof. Opening it helped considerably.

Before the morning was over they had located many donkeys, found a flock of about 200 emus, sighted three camels, and found, on the river-flats, some brumbies.

There was no doubt that Les was a very competent pilot. He handled the machine with an assurance born of long practice and the full knowledge that, in this country and in this type of light plane, there was no margin for error.

Les did not miss much, but it was evident that he appreciated the keen eyes of the boys in the plane. Peter felt a sense of awe that they were able to survey such great tracts of land in so short a time, and felt that he had entered a new dimension, as indeed he had, in relation to the running of this vast station.

It was almost with unbelief, when he glanced at his watch, that he realised they had been in the air for two hours.

Les by now was skirting the river-flats, and he followed the main river-bed for some time, noting any permanent pools which still remained.

From the air, the river-course looked even more beautiful than it did from the ground, with the great, white gums on the banks and, now and again, a long, shaded, clear pool. It was in this area that the station kept its cattle.

"We'll come down here this afternoon," said Les. "Dad wants to have a look at the cattle. You'll find it pretty interesting."

He swept along the roadway leading back to the station. Almost before they knew it, they were dropping down on the runway.

"That was great, Les. We'll come with you any time."

"We've found plenty of work to do," said Les. "This will keep us busy for a while. The fence in Yuna, the mill in Pimba, the dam in Willa, the gate in Hinda—maybe you noticed something else."

"Not me," said Jet. "This is plenty for the time being."

That afternoon they had their first experience with the cattle.

"I'm running cross-breds," Mr Stewart informed them. "We're using Brahmin stock. I think it's going to be a success."

"Aren't the cattle dangerous to handle, Mr Stewart?"

"Some are perhaps—not ours. Every time we go out to them, we take a bale of hay. We mean nice food to them, and they're not frightened of us, even though we don't see them often."

"I'll take you out and you'll find they will eat out of your hand," said Tim, who had come over and heard the conversation."

"*Your* hand," said Peter with emphasis. "I stay in the truck."

"Me too," said Jet. "I've been treed too often."

The men laughed.

"You must have been in the wrong place then. The cattle don't do that here. We treat them with respect and they treat us the same way."

It was, however, with a spirit of scepticism that the boys assisted Mr Stewart to load a few bales of hay on a truck and they set off for the area where the cattle were.

The grass was growing well, and no sheep had been allowed in this particular area for a long time. There was also a great amount of wild life in the area, also attracted by the plentiful feed. There seemed, however, to be a kind of amiable agreement between the domestic animals and the rest to live and let live.

"The cattle need a considerable amount of room in this country just the same," said Mr Stewart when Peter commented on the number feeding together. "Sometimes as much as 100 acres per animal. You can't fool about in this country — overstock and you can't use a paddock for as long as ten years while it recovers."

"How many cattle have you, Mr Stewart?" asked Peter.

"Don't rightly know, son, but we'll come out on the right side. This is not true cattle country, like my holdings further north, but it's a worthwhile experiment. If this country could stand enough cattle, they would be an easier proposition than sheep."

"Don't let dad get on to his favourite topic," said Les as he pulled the truck to a halt.

As they did so the animals near at hand moved towards them. Mr Stewart alighted and held out handfuls of hay as a peace-offering. A number of animals came up and took the offering from him.

In a few moments the truck was surrounded. Peter, too, stepped out and the animals did not resent him.

"You city people get a lot of wrong ideas about the country," said Mr Stewart.

Watching him, Peter could not but agree. Not only had he had a lot of wrong ideas, but in actual fact he now knew that his thinking about modern sheep stations had been based on books written early in the century, or by reading books by Banjo Paterson and Henry Lawson.

Jet offered no comment at all. Perhaps the adaptability that had allowed his Aboriginal ancestors to survive was strong in him, and he could adapt as freely to the new as those in the past could to the old—that was, provided he was given the chance.

As they drove back to the homestead, after inspecting the area and making sure there was plenty of feed and water, Peter began to think about Jet. It was strange, but already the boy was changing, not only in his attitude, but even unconsciously in his speech. He no longer spiced his talk with "seens" and "dones" and other wrong expressions, but had he been told about this he would have indignantly denied that he was any different.

Peter, on the other hand, was learning much from Jet. Things that would have escaped him once were becoming part of his awareness—the ground which revealed like a book to those who could read it what had passed over it, the behaviour of the birds which indicated so many things, the appearance of the sky which showed what kind of day it would be, the lay of the country which showed where water holes might be and, as a result, where many more sheep than usual might be found. He had gained the ability to move and even run for long periods without fatigue, the ability for quick anticipation—these and many other facets of life were becoming part of his nature.

The continuing companionship of those at the station also brought him a new inner strength and a gradual identification with everything about him, so that already he was beginning to share the interest of the adults in the welfare of Yullamooloo.

The attitude of the boy had not escaped the eye of the alert Harry Stewart.

"Captain Thomas Devlin," he mused to himself, "you may be feeling you cannot do a thing for your boy. We'll make a man of him for you and when you come home you'll be proud of him."

Chapter Seven

CLICK GO THE SHEARS

ALMOST BEFORE THEY REALISED IT, the shearing season had begun.

"For the next month," said Mr Stewart, "the sun sets the time. We will have a big team of shearers in the shed and it is our responsibility to keep the supply of sheep up to them. You boys will stay away from the place unless you're invited.

"This team is under the control of old Charlie Carr and he runs the shed while he is here. He's entitled to come up to the house and live with us, but he generally likes to have his own quarters down below. We'll make sure he is comfortable."

Mrs Stewart took over the preparation for the coming of the men by going down to the quarters and supervising the scrubbing of all the rooms, the provision of good bedding, and the placing of the necessary furniture in each room.

"You're got to be careful with these chaps,"

she said. "Make the place too prissy and they object; leave out the things they feel they need and they object even louder. I always leave some extra odds and ends of furniture in a spare room, so that those that want to can make themselves more comfortable. In any case it's their business the way they live once they're here, but we must provide them with a decent place to start with."

They opened up the mess-hut, and with plenty of elbow grease had all the pots and pans gleaming and clean.

"You'd better be careful how you leave the kitchen, May," said Stewart to his wife. "This team has a couple of women cooks."

"Women cooks?" said Peter. "Who ever heard of women cooks in a shearing shed?"

"It's quite the thing now, Peter. The men like it. The grub's much better and the women are much cleaner."

Peter shook his head. He had obviously not been reading the right books about the Outback.

The kitchen was a huge place, with insect-proof windows and doors and an air-conditioner in one wall. The range was a large oil-fired affair, and the pantry was packed full of stores.

The mess-room doubled as a recreation-room, with dartboards and provision for a bar if necessary.

"Most of the fellows prefer to buy their

refreshment from us, and they get through a fair bit. They sweat so much they need constant liquid of some sort or other, with good breaks during the day for tea and food. Keep away from them, unless they invite you down. They bring their own rouseabouts and shed hands, and we'll only intrude when things get too busy. They can be pretty handy with their fists and are pretty touchy after a day's work, so go easy with them."

Over the next few days the team began to assemble. They came in a great variety of old cars and vans. A number towed caravans and apparently had brought their families.

At the same time, several Aboriginal stockmen also came in from Daniel Creek. They too settled down in their own quarters, with a very large Aboriginal woman to cook for them. Jet claimed he was a distant relative and spent all his spare time down with the stockmen.

The shearers' cook proved to be a formidable woman, Mrs Sara Murphy. She was assisted by a meek little woman, the wife of one of the shearers named Taylor. After a first encounter with Mrs Murphy, Peter and Jet gave her a wide berth, and they noticed that even Les and Tim treated her with respect.

She had a penetrating voice, and as she worked she talked loudly, emphasising each word with the crashing of pans on the stove or the heavy sound of cutting when she was doing the vegetables. Mrs Murphy cutting vegetables, talking at the top of her voice, and brandishing her knife in the air for emphasis was a sight not easily forgotten.

She quickly took up a position of authority over the Aboriginal boys sent over to attend to the oil and to keep the bathhouse water hot. Woe betide the unfortunate lad who failed to empty her rubbish bins, or to supply her with what she needed. Even Mr Stewart was not exempt from her wrath when she was put out about something.

If nothing else, the whole area of the kitchen, mess, and quarters under her dominance became a place of virtue, cleanliness, and clean language. She was such a superb cook that everyone was prepared to put up with her domination for the sake of the excellent meals she prepared.

"I've got my boys to look after," she said with emphasis, "and look after them I will. Nothing's too good for them."

To a shearer uninitiated to her ways, the sight of plates of morning-tea sandwiches, garnished with lettuce and other decorations, was a shock. However, there was always more than enough for all, and though they grinned at the embellishments, they ate the sandwiches, and then the shredded lettuce, and decorations as well, with relish.

The Aboriginal cook at the stockmen's quarters preferred to cook outdoors rather than use the kitchen stove provided. Her skill in cooking was no less for this, and many a time as he passed, Peter's mouth watered at the delicious smell of roasting meat that emanated from her open-air fireplace.

On one occasion when Peter wandered over to the quarters with Jet, he looked into some of the rooms and found that in most cases the beds had been pushed aside and the men preferred to use the floors for sleeping. He mentioned this to Les.

"Don't worry. We've provided good quarters and how they use them is their own business. They resent our intrusion as much as we would theirs. They'll make do. Providing they are happy and keep up a good standard of hygiene, they must be allowed to live as they want. They get the same basic rations as anyone here, and their wages are protected by law. We give them plenty of chances of earning extra money, as you will see. They don't do so badly."

Peter found the twelve Aboriginal stockmen a very amiable group, easy to get on with and with a good sense of humour. There was no self-consciousness in them, such as he had noticed with Aborigines in the town. Indeed, they radiated a rugged independence and a sense of dignity which he was glad to see.

The tall, thin woolclasser in charge of the shearers, Charlie Carr, arrived at about the same time too, and installed himself in his quarters. He elected to come up to the homestead for tea the first night, but excused himself from either living there or taking further meals with the family.

Peter was surprised to see with what respect he was treated by the shearers. Perhaps his position of authority gave them a sense of security in that he was capable of watching their interests. For whatever cause, his word was law with everyone.

"We couldn't have it otherwise," said Mr Stewart. "This operation costs us over $10 000, and a poor shearing team would not only waste time and be expensive, but the whole operation would get snarled up. In a short time, every sheep we can find on the property has to be mustered, culled, and shorn. The fleeces must be graded, baled, and transported away. Then we must attend to the sheep, before finally getting them back to their paddocks."

"It must take you months, Mr Stewart."

"Months—no. A month—yes, at the outside. You'll be taking part in the first roundup tomorrow. We bring the first lot in at daybreak."

Les and Tim did not bother about preparing meals for themselves at shearing time. Early next morning, while it was still dark, the four of them went over to the kitchen at the homestead where they found a delicious meal waiting for them.

Mr Stewart had brought a number of friends from the town to assist in the various activities, and a large number sat round the huge table.

"Les will do the spotting," said Mr Stewart, "and Tim will work with the stockmen. Peter can go up with Les, and Jet can help Tim on the ground with the truck. We've checked all the radios, and all the bikes are ready with their own walkie-talkies."

Peter and Les walked over to find a truck to go down to the airstrip. Already there was a roar of engines from the bike shed, and as he watched, Peter saw each of the stockmen leaving.

Seated on each bike was a fine-looking Aboriginal stockman. Each man handled his machine like a veteran, as he took it slowly on to the road. On each back was slung a walkie-talkie, and on each pillion sat an alert sheep dog, completely at home on his perch and in no way in danger of being dislodged. In addition, on each tank a second dog sat, looking eager to go, and quite at home on the machine.

As the sun came up, it showed a long line of

men on their bikes, riding down the road to the plain.

"Come on," called Les, settling behind the wheel of the truck. "We've got to get out and get the sheep moving."

They drove along the road, passing the line of bikes, and were soon at the airstrip.

The aeroplane had been serviced the night before, and they wheeled it out of the hangar.

"You'd better come up to the front seat," said Les, "but don't touch the controls whatever you do. I try to keep a margin of safety, but as you'll see, we come down a bit low at times."

The machine started up immediately and they taxied to the end of the strip. In a few moments they were airborne.

Below they could see a long cloud of dust, where the stockmen were making their way to their agreed positions.

"We've got enough to start with in Winga," said Les. "It's not far out, and they should have the first mob in by midmorning. The shearers can begin tomorrow if they want to."

Les took the plane to the far extremity of the fence line, and made a dive at the ground, the siren going full blast. The effect was startling, as scores of sheep came into view, moving at a run before them.

He made a number of sweeps, and then

radioed to those on the ground. Looking down, Peter could see Tim and Jet standing by the four-wheel-drive, with a radio on the bonnet.

It was a matter-of-fact conversation, and in a few words all below were aware of the position. Jet moved off towards the stockmen, now some distance down the road. Les brought the plane overhead and circled.

The bikes stopped, and further instructions were given. The stockmen moved off into the scrub. Streaks of dust showed where the dogs were keeping the sheep moving in the desired direction.

Les banked the plane over another paddock. On one tight turn, Peter caught his breath as he glanced down and saw that the edge of the wing seemed to be almost scraping the ground.

There was such an air of assurance about Les's deft handling of the plane, however, that Peter was not worried about crashing. Nevertheless it would take very little, he knew, for them to dip the wing into the ground and meet disaster.

On the ground Jet was glad he was riding a bike and not spotting from the plane. As it moved overhead with its siren screaming, and then suddenly turned, with its wing dipped to the ground, it did not appear at any time that there was enough clearance for it to pass between the trees. At times it disappeared from view at what appeared to be treetop level, and only the sound of its engine showed it was still airborne.

It was, however, achieving its purpose. Already the sheep were grouping and, acting on the general directions, Jet swung his bike behind a mob and edged them towards the northern fence where even larger mobs were building up.

The old bush balladists might have been revolving in their graves at the methods of the modern stockmen, but their hearts would still have rejoiced at the magnificent spectacle the mustering presented as it progressed.

The early morning sun had cast an orange glow over the ground and the trees, and the dust, rising from the hundreds of hooves, caught the light so that the air itself appeared to be afire with orange.

Then the mobs joined together, making the whole area into a moving mass of dust-brown, woolly fleeces. Every now and again, a small group attempted to break away. This was quickly stopped by the score or more of sheep dogs, which now ringed the flock. With much barking, pretence at snapping, and occasionally even running over the backs of the sheep, the dogs were slowly but surely driving the entire mob in the direction of the shearing shed.

Even Jet paused in astonishment at the rare

beauty of the scene, when the sheep moved down a small dip to cross a dry creek and then up the other side. At that moment, in the reflected light of the early-morning sun, every sheep appeared to have a fleece of gold.

Meanwhile Les returned to the strip, and he and Peter put the plane into the hangar.

"One day I'll give you a chance to handle the controls, Peter, but not during shearing," he said.

They took the truck and moved over towards the holding yards near the shearing sheds.

Mr Stewart was already there, assisting in the culling of the sheep as they came in. Those with sub-standard fleeces were set aside in a special pen. In due course they would be slaughtered to provide rations for the station.

It was dusty work getting the sheep through the drafting gates. The animals were stubborn and had to be prodded and assisted along the narrow runs. The men shouted, beat tins, rattled bottle tops in other tins, and kept up such a din that eventually even the most reluctant animal went where it was wanted.

Next morning, with the full quota of shearers hard at work, Charlie Carr called for some extra casual labour in the shed. Stewart sent Peter and Jet in.

Jet fitted in immediately, but it was soon evident that Peter was lagging on the job.

Some of the shearers swore at him for not being fast enough in removing a fleece, and when he threw it on the skirting table, he made a mess of it too, and had the skirters angry with him also.

There were two sixteen-year-old boys in the team named Clarrie Reddin and Mick Coffey. Taking their cue they began to annoy Peter, and did everything to impede him. Jet watched this for a while, but bided his time, until on one occasion when one of the "smart Alecs" was making a rush to the table with a fleece, Jet dropped his broom in front of him, causing the other lad to trip.

The boy slipped on to the floor, uttering a string of oaths and calling Jet a filthy nigger.

As one, Peter and Jet attacked him, but his mate came up from behind, and with two mighty swipes knocked Peter to one end of the shed and Jet to the other.

They skidded down between the shearers, causing great confusion and further profanity. Carr, always alert to the possibility of trouble, switched off the motor driving the shearing blades and called out, "Throw the four of them out."

A dozen eager hands grabbed the boys and they found themselves flying through the door in to the dust outside.

Jet was on his feet first and flew into his

original opponent. Peter, not far behind, took a flying tackle at his.

The shearers, in the meantime, had all come out of the shed, while Mr Stewart and the others from the drafting yards also came running. They were in time to see Jet, though much smaller than his attacker, pounding him to such a degree that the lad gave ground and eventually ran out of the ring behind the shearers. He was thrust back roughly, only to be met with such an onslaught that he flung himself to the ground and remained there.

Peter was not faring as well and, deciding that he had neither the height nor the weight to stand up to the boy fighting him, ran instead under his guard and put a wrestling hold on him. They fell to the ground in a cloud of dust, with arms, legs, elbows, and teeth all being used to good effect.

Stewart waited till they had battered each other to the stage that honour should have been satisfied, and then nodded to the men to prise them apart.

Charlie Carr lifted up his two fighters and booted them back through the door. Stewart grabbed Jet and Peter and did the same. They all rolled in a heap amid the wool bales, all breath and fight knocked out of them.

They untangled themselves.

"Anyone want to make anything more out of

it?" asked the largest of the boys, rising and rubbing himself. "That Carr's got a kick like a mule."

"Not me," said Peter, also rising and dusting himself down. "Old Stewart used to be a footballer. He's still got a mighty right foot."

"Who's a filthy nigger?" asked Jet rising and confronting his opponent.

"Sorry, mate. I opened my big mouth too wide."

"Good," said Jet. "Keep it closed in future and we'll all get on."

In this way a sort of peace was declared and, though Peter had two black eyes for a few days, a kind of respect grew up between them all from then on.

By now the number of sheep which had been shorn demanded their attention. The animals had to be inspected for cuts and wounds, dipped, and finally driven up long ramps to the huge, double-decker semi-trailer which was to take them to their new pastures fifty kilometres away. It was all done with a process-line efficiency that amazed Peter.

"Do you lose many?" he asked when, with the transporter fully loaded, he was assigned with Tim to take them away.

"As long as we don't lose more than we breed, we're okay. We estimate we lose about 5000 a year through natural causes, mainly old age. We gain somewhere near 6000, so that suits us. If we get too many, we overstock, and we have to sell some. That's how we picked up this place originally. The previous owner got greedy, overstocked, lost good feed areas, and then he couldn't carry on."

Tim was an excellent driver. The other members of the family predicted a short life and a sudden end to the great vehicle he handled, but when Peter had done a few trips with him, he realised that the young man's love of machinery and his devotion in the care of this huge diesel-engined vehicle was something which would confound his critics.

They were taking over 1000 sheep a day out to their new feeding grounds. On one trip, they passed an old hut with a stack of beer bottles higher than the hut itself.

"That used to be a boundary rider's hut," said Tim. "Nowadays we just couldn't use the kind of labour they had in the old days—down-and-outs, many of them living on a wage which barely supplied rations, and native stockmen paid a pittance or not at all. That's why we have to speed things up—move the sheep out by truck, do our surveying by air, run the sheep through the yards in one great process. We live on the edge of a razor blade as it is; sometimes the price of wool is low, and sometimes it reaches fantastic heights."

Chapter Eight

SOME LESSONS FROM THE EXPERT

DURING ALL THIS TIME there was no time to think of football, and neither boy expected to be free to leave the station for at least a month.

However, Harry Stewart himself came to the bungalow one evening after the boys had finished work and were resting after a shower.

"I've arranged for a truck to go to town on Saturday," he told them, "and you both can go with it and return on Saturday night. In the meantime, if you like to come over after tea, I'll light up the tennis courts and show you a few points."

Jet was the more excited of the two.

"Funny to think that a bloke out of the scrap book I used to have is real. He was the greatest. I bet we're pretty lucky."

"He's probably getting a bit too old to remember too much," said the more practical Peter, "and don't forget, things have changed a bit since his day."

"A ball's a ball, and a foot's a foot," said

Jet. "I don't know any of our blokes these days who kicked further or more accurately than the boss."

"It'll be good just the same," Peter conceded. "He certainly takes an interest in us."

The workouts on the tennis courts surprised both boys. They had quite a large area to move around, as six courts had originally been provided for. Even Tim and Les were attracted to come over, and provide some opposition for the boys.

To their surprise, Harry Stewart appeared to have lost none of his cunning in regard to the game.

"I often think," he remarked, "that these days some of our Australian Rules fellows think they're playing rugby and should burst their way through for a touchdown. All they use is brute force and over-hard knocks."

"I've learnt to take the knocks," said Peter.

"Maybe, but there are many you can avoid."

"How?"

"Specialise in propping, dodging, dummying, and so on. Have such a variety of tricks up your sleeve that you'll always have your opposite number guessing. It's pretty play too, fellows, and is a lot more than just bulldozing ability."

So it went on, and from it all the boys learned much. Every now and again Peter dropped in a question or two relating to the old game.

"What would happen if I decided to take a place-kick for goal?"

"I think you'd be shot. It was a survival from the early days, and slowed the game down. Personally I liked the place-kick. It kept the crowd on its toes waiting for the final result, and done well it looked very good."

"Doesn't seem to work very well in rugby," observed Jet. "They don't convert very often."

"I refuse to comment further," said Harry Stewart with a smile, "or Tim won't speak to me for a week."

"Everyone to his own tastes," said Tim. "After all, rugby is a man's game."

Harry Stewart was standing about five metres away holding the ball.

Yelling out, "Stop this, young Tim," he launched the ball straight at Tim's chest with his good leg. The force of the ball was so great that it knocked the young man backwards on to the ground, and the ball bounced off the courts.

"Sorry, old fellow," said Stewart, with mock contrition, helping his son to his feet, "I see your point. Australian Rules is definitely not your game."

"Rotten old cow," said Tim, also with a grin, "I'd like to have you on the rugby field for five minutes."

May Stewart, watching from the verandah, thought to herself, "Boys will be boys, and when it comes to football, Harry is the biggest boy of the lot round here."

Peter and Jet were delighted with the byplay, but tried not to show it. To them these practices became something to be looked forward to and enjoyed to the full. From each they were gaining more than they knew.

Chapter Nine

JET JACKS UP

THE SHEARING SEASON CONTINUED its inevitable course, with the greatest number of sheep being rounded up during the first few weeks. Les needed to make longer and longer surveys in the plane to seek out the less easily found stock.

On the river-flats, once the sheep were found, the rest was easy. When, however, the activities moved to the hills, there were so many gullies and ravines for the sheep to move into, that even the plane became useless for spotting, and it was necessary to send the stockmen in with their bikes to cover every bit of the country.

At times the teams became so split up that it was only by frequent calls on their radios that they avoided moving over previously covered ground, and made sure that no parts were missed.

"Each fleece is worth anything up to ten dollars," Harry Stewart reminded them. "Even when you've got the main mob in, it will pay you to go out with the big truck and round up the stragglers."

The result was that in the last week parties were out looking for any sheep that had been missed previously. The shearers had work waiting on other stations and would leave the job if there was no longer enough sheep being brought in for them to complete their daily tally. It was therefore essential that the sheep be kept up to them.

Already the Aboriginal stockmen were becoming restless. They knew that by now they had earned enough in wages to keep them in comfort for a fairly long time in the town and they became more selective in what extra work they would or would not do, irrespective of payment.

This irritated Mr Stewart, but there was nothing he could do about it but call on the boys and his own family to carry out the extra work. This could be anything from bringing in a load of wood, and keeping the bathhouse water hot in the shearing quarters, to moving out to the more remote areas, combing the scrub for the stragglers.

As a result, Peter and Jet covered much more of the station than they did usually. Both were observant, and they were soon well versed in the various areas when they were discussed round the table at breakfast or tea.

One day Les returned after a sweep in the plane and said, "I've found something, I think, in Devil's Gorge, but it's too risky to observe and pilot at the same time. There shouldn't be any sheep there. The area is well fenced off, but I'm sure I saw movement."

Les took off again with Jet aboard as observer. The plane returned over two hours later. Les was in a rage and came stamping into the homestead.

"That blasted Jet," he stormed. "He jacked up on me. I ran down the gorge a number of times, and I'm sure I disturbed quite a lot of sheep, but I couldn't make a count while flying the plane. He absolutely refused to co-operate. I don't know if there are enough sheep out there to justify taking the semi-trailer out, but I'm going out again tomorrow with some men and bikes."

Early next morning, Les took a large four-wheel-drive truck and had the boys help him load several bikes on it.

"We'll take a number of the stockmen and the dogs," he said, "and Jet, Tim, and Peter can make up the party."

As they were loading, Jet sidled up close to Peter.

"Don't go," he said.

"Why not?"

"Don't go. I warn you."

"Don't be silly. You seem to have gone round the bend all of a sudden."

However, when it was time to start, Jet was missing and no amount of searching could find him.

"Something seems to have bitten him," said Les. "We won't worry about him. Hop on, everyone. We'll pick up the stockmen on the way out."

When they reached the Aborigines' quarters, no one was there except the large cook.

"Where is everyone?" asked Les.

"Some go here; some go somewhere else. Don't ask me," she replied.

Les took the truck back to the homestead and picked up some of the men working round the machine shop. There was still not an Aboriginal to be seen. On the way out Peter questioned Les about the area.

"We don't know much about the country round the range," said Les. "We intend to run cattle there one day. With proper development we could hold the water that falls on the hills. There are some artesian wells there too. If we spent a bit of money the area could produce just about anything."

"Have you ever explored Devil's Gorge?" asked Peter.

"No. We've never had any reason to up till now. Judging by the way the sheep have made tracks for it, there must be plenty of water there."

"Why is it called Devil's Gorge?"

"Nothing significant as far as I know. The Aboriginal name for this range is Minn-narie, which means mountain devil, and when we saw the place from the air originally, we just called it Devil's Gorge to distinguish it on the map and to place it in its right location."

It was a long journey to the gorge. Before they went towards the foothills, Les took the truck along the fence as far as he could, and then Tim and Peter each mounted a bike and rode on.

Under a clump of trees, where it could not be seen from the air, a length of fence had been ripped out, either by cattle trying to get in or by goats or donkeys trying to get out.

Judging by the churned up appearance of the ground, it was obvious that a large number of sheep had moved through the fence towards the gorge.

"There's plenty of water there," said Tim, "but this is cattle country and we try and keep the sheep right off it. Les was right. He must have seen plenty of movement. There could be a hundred sheep out there."

They rode back along the fence to the truck to collect the others. With Les in the lead, they then all rode their bikes over the country-side, following the sheep's hoofprints.

Geologically the hills forming the range were very old. The forces of nature had twisted them and then weathered them so that now they sometimes stood in stark formations, with great vertical walls of rock, rising abruptly from the plains.

"Be careful where you go," warned Les as they pulled up at the entrance to the gorge. "This place has apparently some significance to Jet and his mob, or they'd have been out with us. Don't touch anything, and ride carefully. All we want to do is get the sheep back. If they reckon this is a sacred spot, I'm not going to argue with them."

The sides reared steeply and sharply above them, so that soon they expected to find they had come to the end of the cleft and to find in front of them a final great impassable wall.

Instead, to their surprise, it suddenly widened into a wide valley, encompassed on all sides by the same high walls, but filled with thick vegetation and broad patches of green.

They had brought with them their usual team of dogs, and at this stage Les stopped and the dogs jumped to the ground.

"I think we'd do better if we left the bikes here," he suggested, "and let the dogs go. There's no doubt there are sheep in here, but we'll have to get among the trees to get them out."

They set the bikes up on the stands, and taking their walkie-talkies they set off on each side of the valley in two parties.

The dogs were restless for action and in a few minutes Les sent them off. The result was quite startling. From one area alone, hundreds of sheep came running down the valley. As the morning continued and they penetrated even further, droves and droves of sheep were found, hundreds and hundreds with long tails, and even many two- and three-year-olds, that obviously had never been mustered before.

It was a bonus that even Les and Tim had not expected. They were very pleased that with a few hours work over a thousand sheep had been found and there were obviously more.

Peter had enjoyed the new experience of moving through the gorge to its greatest extremity, where a huge pool, fed from a cascade of water from the cliffs above, showed why the sheep had made a break for this particular area.

On the way he walked a little higher up, and closer to the great walls than the others. In the distance, he could hear the barkings of the dogs and the noise of the men shouting and the sheep protesting as they were driven down the valley.

He too would have moved down, but his attention was caught by a narrow split in the rock wall. He turned to examine it to see if it led into perhaps another valley which might also hold some sheep, but there was no evidence that any had recently passed this way. Just the same, beneath his feet was a firmly beaten track and, as he followed it, he found the cleft began to widen until suddenly it ran into a wide bowl of a sizeable area.

The space was clear of vegetation, but in places rocks had been piled in strange formations, obviously by some human agency. He walked on until he was standing in the middle of the area. Around him were a number of large caves, so dark that he could not see within them.

He felt a strange, eerie sensation. There was no doubt he had stumbled on the site of an Aboriginal meeting place. The reason why Jet and the Aboriginal stockmen had refused to come to the gorge was now clear.

What lay within the caves he could only conjecture. He felt sure that inside they would yield a store of material to make the heart of an anthropologist jump for joy.

For a moment he felt the urge to run forward, but suddenly he remembered the look on Jet's face.

"Don't go," the boy had said. Looking back, Peter realised that it was more an entreaty to a friend than a command.

He stood for a moment, and then slowly walked back the way he had come. He rejoined the others, but did not mention where he had been or what he had seen. Instead he said, "I've covered the east side of the gorge right up to the side. There are no sheep there."

By now they had the sheep out on the plains and were again on their bikes. Les rode back to the truck and sent a radio call to the station asking for the big semi-trailer to be sent out.

By late afternoon they had taken all the sheep to the station, and had repaired the fence. It had been a long, tiring day and Peter was glad to get back finally to his quarters and have a cleanup.

Peter sought out Mr Stewart.

"Please don't blame Jet for not going out this morning," he said. "He had good reasons."

Mr Stewart was not very sympathetic.

"He wasn't the only one. What did they expect to find out there—dragons?"

"I don't know, Mr Stewart, but did you know that Jet has been initiated?"

"Probably has. Round these parts they take the young bucks and do it, whether they want it or not, if they get the chance. Pretty painful and puts them off work for a bit. We used to have a lot of trouble when the Aborigines lived on the property, and I suppose it still goes on."

"No, that isn't a correct initiation, Mr

Stewart. Jet was brought up in the city most of his life, but his father reclaimed him when his foster-mother died. He went through the proper initiation in all its details. That's why he's so mixed up. He still isn't sure what he is—an Aboriginal or a white boy. The initiation must have impressed him. He still talks of being an Aboriginal, while he tries to be like me."

"He certainly is mixed up," said Stewart. "I was annoyed with him this morning, but I understand a bit more now, though I'll never fully understand those people. You can tell him he's not in strife. In any case he turned up after you'd left and did a good day's work. So did the others, but I think they'd have nipped off for good if they hadn't had to wait for their pay."

Peter sought out Jet. He found him that evening having tea with the Aboriginal stockmen. Peter had established a good relationship with them and they did not resent his being around.

The men were squatting around drinking their beer ration with their food. Peter decided to come right to the point.

"I'm sorry about today," he said, talking to them all.

"It's none of your business," said one of the men, a very large fellow who seemed to speak for them all.

"That's quite right. That's what Jet told me after he got into trouble refusing to 'spot' over the gorge."

"The boss doesn't understand," said another. "That place is none of his business."

"It's on his property," said Peter, "but if you'd been sensible about it, there would have been no trouble."

"What do you mean?"

"Why not come out and explain that your people regard it as a special place."

The men all laughed. "It won't remain special too long. Blokes will come out and take photos. It'll get in the papers and then everyone will come."

"Well, I'll tell you something," said Peter. "Les Stewart was mighty particular how he had us get the sheep out. He understands how you feel about it."

"Les ain't bad. He'd do that. But other blokes talk."

"Nobody found anything," said Peter. "I'll swear that. I watched all the time."

"What are you trying to be—a white do-gooder for us poor Aborigines," said one of the men in a mocking tone of voice.

Peter flushed. He knew he was intruding on dangerous ground. It was Jet who came to his rescue.

"Leave him alone," he said. "He won't tell

anything, even if he knows anything to tell."

"He'd better not," came a voice from the darkness.

"He's okay. He's ignorant like the rest of them about our mob, but he won't do no harm."

Peter turned to Jet.

"You're not in strife with the boss, Jet. He told me to tell you. He understands a lot. Perhaps he doesn't understand completely, but when you're in trouble he'd be the first to help."

"We don't need any help—beer and wages and goodbye," said the big man. "And that is goodbye to you too, young fellow."

"I'm sorry," said Peter. "I only wanted to help."

"Then go away; that will help," said the same mocking voice from the darkness. "Your mob have been helping us for ages and look at us."

Peter turned and walked away. The fat woman was still at her pots and pans at the open fireplace as he went by.

"You're a nice boy, sonny," she called, as he walked past her. "Don't take them too seriously. They wouldn't know what they wanted if you asked them."

Jet caught him up, just before he reached the bungalow. The boy's breath smelt of drink and he was a little tipsy.

"Peter," he called. Peter stopped.

"I don't know which way to go," said Jet. "I'm all muddled up."

"This way," said Peter pointing to the bungalow. "You'll have a whale of a hangover in the morning, but nobody's after you."

The boy stood indecisively in the darkness for a moment. Peter too stopped. It was a moment of truth for both of them.

A slim form slipped past him. He heard the door of the bungalow bang. He heard the door of the inner bedroom bang.

Peter sat down on a log to try to work things out, but no answers came.

When he too entered the quarters the loud snores from Jet's bedroom showed that he was back in the fold for that night at least.

A Latin expression he had learnt at school came to Peter's mind: Quo Vadis? Whither goest thou? "Neither of us knows," he thought. "We've both got problems, but his are greater than mine."

Chapter Ten

JOE WILSON READS THE LESSON

WHILE ALL THIS HAD BEEN going on, Peter was gradually able to repay his friends who had assisted him along the way. His original leaving of the city had been due to the kindness of the mother of a friend of his from school and, as he received his wages, he put enough aside so that very soon he had the satisfaction of being able to repay her in full.

He was able to pay Jack Williams for the new clothes he had bought on credit from him. Mr Williams was aware of the location of his old friend, Joe Wilson, who had also lent him money, and it was with pleasure that he was able not only to repay the old shearer, but to tell him there would be plenty of casual work for him at Yullamooloo after the shearers left, if he wanted it.

During this time too, the boys had played their usual weekend football matches, with varying results. They were both leg weary and trying over-hard, and though each boy played himself to a standstill in each match, Bill Langforth could see that they would not settle down till later in the season, and dropped Peter from one of the matches.

As a result, Jet played a very poor game and the team lost. It was a valuable lesson to the coach and the boys. Too much depended on both of them, and Langforth took the opportunity to bring this home to the other members of the team.

"The combination of Mercedes and Devlin has been winning us matches," he pointed out. "When they slump, the whole team slumps. It's nice to have outstanding kids, but they must be backed up by the entire team."

Coming when it did, the circumstances were a shock to both Peter and Jet—Peter to realise how cocky he was becoming on the football field, and Jet to realise that he was part of a combination, and that when Peter was missing he was at a loss.

They did not get any consolation from Harry Stewart, though he well understood their feelings. However, as the shearing was almost finished and Les was also wanting to get back to the squash courts, he let them resume their midweek trips to town for practice.

There was enough work for the stockmen for a few days, but when the shearing team indicated that there were not enough sheep coming in to hold them at the station, the Aborigines left immediately, after a gigantic binge on all their remaining beer rations.

Jet compensated by keeping very close to Peter, and the boy felt that at least for the time being Jet was now identifying himself with him and the station people.

Then one day, with the usual clattering, banging, and crashing, Joe Wilson arrived. Peter heard the familiar sound of his vintage car coming up the escarpment road and, yelling out to Jet to come, rushed out to meet his remarkable old friend.

The great high vehicle came to a halt, with its usual cloud of dust and steam, in the middle of the station yard. Joe stepped out, his usual hairy, fuzzy self, gave his trousers a hitch, and watched the boys running to him.

"Bless me!" he said, looking around at the magnificent homestead and the two boys, a vivid contrast to what they were when he had last seen them at Boolgana Downs. "No less than Mr Devlin and Mr Mercedes Benz."

"Jet Mercedes," Peter corrected him. "We've both gone classy since you saw us last, and it's all thanks to you."

Attracted by the clatter, Mr Stewart walked over. Judging by the excitement of the boys, he needed no second guess as to who the man was.

"Glad to have you, Joe," he said. "The boys give you a good recommendation. We've quite a lot of strays to keep you busy for some time—you can work on a pay-weekly basis, or so much per hundred."

"You leave it to us," boasted Jet. "You'll do better on what we bring in. There's enough strays to keep you here for months."

"Doesn't speak too well for you fellows on the mustering," said Stewart, "but the boys are right, Joe. You'll have plenty to do."

When it came to the matter of quarters, Joe elected to provide for himself. "The boys can help out now and then," he said. "We've worked pretty well together before."

"Take him away and make him comfortable," said Mr Stewart to Peter and Jet.

They stood on the running boards of the car and directed Joe back to the shearers' quarters, now empty and untidy.

In no time they had found him a comfortable room, had opened up the kitchen again, and had him sitting talking to them with a large mug of tea in his hand. There was so much to tell him and so much he had to learn of their good fortune at Yullamooloo.

"I met Captain Williams, my old army boss," he told them, "and he's got a bit of good news about your dad, Peter. Some Peace Group or other was in North Vietnam recently and they reported having seen him alive and well."

"My friends in the city wrote and told me he was alive, but I haven't heard anything else. He's going to be mighty grateful to you, Joe, when he comes home."

"Nuts," said Joe. "Anyone would have helped you. You seem to have fallen on your feet here."

"What happened to old Josh McMichael?" Peter asked, referring to his former boss at the run-down Boolgana station.

"Don't rightly know. I went out there a few days after you left. I'd decided to pick you up, come what may. He was busy extracting his tractor from inside his house."

He looked at the boys.

"Can't rightly say that was a very nice thing to do boys."

"I did it," said Jet. "Peter had nothing to do with it. I deliberately ran his tractor into his house to pay him out. I wouldn't do it now, but it seemed the right thing to do then."

"You didn't do much damage fortunately—busted a wall in, and put the tractor in the middle of his living-room. But he didn't have anything much in it, as you know. It was a pigsty. Getting the tractor out was his greatest problem as it had gone through the floor. He managed it in the end, and patched up the place with a few sheets of corrugated iron."

The boys' enthusiasm at having their old friend with them was such that they would have moved down to the shearing quarters with him. Joe put an end to that idea.

"Nope. I'm a bloke that likes a bit of peace and quiet, and you two young bucks would be too much for me. You make the most of what you've got. I ain't no example to young folk."

Over the next week, even Harry Stewart was surprised at the number of strays the boys brought in. Joe was kept fully busy, all day and every day, and Stewart considered the old man a good bargain. Over 1000 sheep came in during the first week, and they found it difficult to find enough feeding grounds for them near the station, while Joe worked through them at the rate of 100 a day.

In this time the boys probably worked harder than they had ever worked before, but as they were doing it for a purpose, they did it with a will every moment of the day.

They took the usual midweek break to go to town and were glad to see that, despite the extra work they were doing, they were regaining their old form on the football field.

On the second week's visit, Peter was surprised to see Jet going to the post office, but, as the boy did not choose to explain what he was doing, Peter did not ask him.

That night after practice Peter returned

first from the shower-room to the dressing-room. Jet had, as usual, left his clothes scattered on the floor.

Peter stooped to pick them up and put them on the bench out of the dampness.

As he did so, a number of pieces of paper on the floor attracted his attention. They might have come from Jet's pockets and so Peter picked them up.

One of them was a money order dated that day. The sender was Jet Mercedes. The address was, "Josh McMichael, Boolgana Downs." The message was, "Pay $30."

Peter stuffed the paper back into Jet's pocket, feeling guilty at what he had seen.

Chapter Eleven

ALL WORK AND SOME PLAY

IT SOON BECAME APPARENT that the boys were so effective in the combing out of the stragglers that old Joe would be almost a permanent resident at the station. So many animals in the home paddocks posed a problem, and in the end Harry Stewart had to enlist the help of old Larry Smith, the carpenter, to help Joe in the sheds. He had tried to get another man or two out, but there was no labour available.

John Angus was also given a respite from his road-grading so that he could help at the sheds. As each man had in the past been a shearer, the daily output rose, if not to very remarkable heights, at least towards the 200 mark a day.

Les was a qualified woolclasser and took over this side of the work. Harry Stewart was very pleased. He had reckoned that the extra sheep the boys were bringing in would raise his clip value by over $10000, even with extra bonuses to all concerned.

In time, the tempo of the station gradually slackened. The two boys found themselves with plenty of energy, even at the end of each day, and put in every minute they could working at their football.

Daniel Creek teams were well in the running for the Central District Premiership, both the Juniors and the Seniors, and the townsfolk were watching them even at practice.

In the Junior Grade a great deal would depend on Jet. He had now developed into an outstanding rover, with pace, stamina, and accuracy. Peter used to watch him spending hours perfecting his accuracy by running at two large, empty, oil drums, set only a few metres apart, and peppering the narrow opening from every angle, no matter how impossible.

Between them, Peter and Jet had perfected a type of play which generally left their opponents floundering. Jet found the crowds applauding him, and twisting his name from its original context to infer he really was jet-propelled when on the field.

The district had its Senior Grade and Junior Grade football. In most clubs the Juniors acted as a reserve team for the Seniors. As a result, Junior teams were made up of boys from about fourteen years, with a wide variation in size and weight.

This had its advantages and disadvantages,

but it meant that sometimes one met a much superior opponent who was standing down from the Senior Grade.

The teams travelled long distances to play their matches, and used grounds which varied from the green grass of Daniel Creek to the hard, stony surface of the cleared area that the people of Kyeema called their oval.

It so happened that this year the Daniel Creek Seniors and Juniors were both playing in the finals of their respective grades on the coming Saturday.

Peter's team was playing Kyeema who were better set up than Daniel Creek in that its Senior Team had not made the finals.

"They'll need a bit of watching," Bill Langforth had warned them. "They'll swing an extra man or two down from their Senior Team, if we don't check every one that they put on the field."

The finals were to be played at the neutral town of Willalong, which lay at an equal distance from Daniel Creek and Kyeema.

During the week before the big match, Harry Stewart spent every spare moment with the boys, and even came over to the bungalow each night to make sure they were in bed early and not staying up late playing cards with Les or Tim. On Friday, when the final was only twenty-four hours away, he checked their football boots with the utmost care, while Mrs Stewart made sure that their blue-and-gold jerseys were fully repaired with their numbers strongly sewn on.

"You'd think Harry was playing tomorrow," Mrs Stewart remarked to Les and Tim. "I've not seen him so interested in the football finals for years."

"Yes, he thinks the sun shines out of both those kids when they're on the football field," said Les, "but neither of them has very much, so they're entitled to a little extra attention now and again."

"Seconded," remarked Tim. "It's against my principles to watch an Australian Rules game but I'm actually going over myself to see their match."

After lunch Harry Stewart came over to the bungalow. He had given the boys the afternoon off, and they were standing under a tree doing some hand passes.

"I want you two kids dressed in your best, with an overnight bag fully packed, over at the house in an hour."

The boys looked at him in surprise.

"Mrs Stewart and I are taking the plane to Willalong this afternoon. Les is piloting us and Tim is coming too."

"Tim! We thought he hated Australian Rules."

"Tim likes you both more. Now get moving."

"By gee," said Jet, "if we lose the game now I'll go and jump in the lake."

"I'll be right with you boy. Come on. We've not that much time."

It was the first time the boys had ridden in Mr Stewart's executive plane. The aircraft, a twin-engined Cessna Golden Eagle, had a passengers' section divided off from the pilots' compartment, and Les and Tim went up forward to take over the controls. The cabin was pressurised, and the plane had a service ceiling of 9700 metres. It had a maximum sea-level speed of 455 km/h.

There were six seats in the main cabin with special arrangements for writing desks. At the rear was a small galley, with hot water and freezing compartments for food.

Peter and Jet lay back in the comfortable seats, and after the plane had taken off looked down on the country as it moved away beneath them.

It was a remarkable kind of life they were leading and one that, even in the good days when he was at school and his family at home, he had never dreamed that it was possible for him to live.

That Stewart was a wealthy man in terms of possessions Peter had no doubt, but in his manner of life and his enjoyment of it, the fineness of the man had not been lost.

Stewart was a man who always "thought big," but with it there was no desire to show off. To take two boys in an executive aircraft to play a football match which would not stir a ripple beyond the confines of the district itself, might appear to some to be the height of absurdity, or to others to be gross one-upmanship.

Not so to Harry Stewart. If all he had owned was a horse and buggy, they would have travelled that way. The fact that they were travelling in a powerful and expensive aircraft was as natural to him as was his modern thinking about running Yullamooloo sheep station.

They landed at the town airport before dark and took a taxi into town. They booked in at a hotel, where the boys shared a room and were told to be ready for tea.

Peter expected that they would be given a dollar or so and sent off down town to get a meal. He and Jet were therefore somewhat surprised when Mrs Stewart banged on the door and said, "Five minutes to tea."

"What does she mean?" asked Jet. "We're not going to eat with them, surely?"

"Don't know," said Peter, "but we'd better look our best." They both had good mops of hair, which Joe had insisted on trimming the night before with his wool shears.

"I don't hold with all that hair," he said, "but if you must wear it, wear it neat."

They had each watched him operate on the other, ready to protest if he cut too deeply, but they had to admit that he had done quite a good job.

They brushed their hair back over their ears, and went out to find the Stewarts.

"In here," said Stewart, opening a glass door. "I'm turning it on for tonight. Celebrating in advance."

"What do I do?" whispered Jet to Peter. "I've never been in one of these joints."

"Do what I do," said Peter. "I don't know the whole drill, but I'll watch the boss."

Considering everything, they did very well, usually managing to use the right implement for the right dish, even Jet gaining confidence towards the end. Though sometimes unaware of what they were eating, they enjoyed it all thoroughly.

"Do some people eat like this all the time?" asked Jet.

"Yes, plenty."

"Heck. They must get awful indigestion," said Peter, stifling an impulse to belch, from the unusual fare.

After tea the boys took a walk through the streets.

It was the largest town either had seen for

some time. The bright lights, the constant movement of traffic, the coming and going of dozens of people, all were sweet to them.

They had gone about a hundred metres along the main road when, to their surprise, they saw advancing towards them their erstwhile opponents of the shearing shed. While on the job, after their fight, an armed truce had existed between them, but it was apparent that this was to be no friendly meeting.

Peter and Jet moved over to the outside of the pavement and the other two did likewise. None was prepared to give way and they stood facing each other, neither side yielding. Peter was alert for a quick swing from one of them, but this did not happen.

How long they would have stayed like this was hard to say, but an impatient man wanting to get to his car pushed them all aside, and in the confusion Peter and Jet slipped on along the street. The other fellows did not attempt to follow, and the incident appeared to be over.

Having reached the end of the shopping complex, both boys turned to go back. They felt that they should get back to the hotel and have an early night.

"We'll have a milk shake and then go to bed," suggested Peter. They found a small shop and, after drinking a malted milk each, set off in the direction of the hotel.

There were not so many people about as before, but down near the hotel they noticed their two tormentors coming up the street towards them, followed by about three or four youths of their own age.

Peter and Jet continued on but, not wishing to cause trouble or possibly get hurt at this important time, they decided it would be more discreet to cross to the other footpath.

There was no doubt that something was intended, for as they did so, the other group also moved over.

"I don't like the look of this," said Peter. "Don't tangle with them, Jet. There are more than we can handle."

Peter began to recross the road. As he did so, he heard a voice cry, "Get them!"

"Get moving," yelled Peter, "to the hotel round the back streets."

The boys turned and ran, only to hear the pounding of feet behind them. Peter was ahead, with Jet bringing up the rear, but he could sense that the others were gaining upon them.

He glanced behind to see the leader taking a grab at Jet. As he did so, Jet dropped to the ground and the fellow, carried on by his own impetus, tripped over the prone boy and went flying into the gutter.

Jet was on his feet in a second and, by the time the next pursuer came to the fallen youth,

Peter and Jet had turned the next corner and had entered the hotel.

"Phew, that was nasty. I think we'd better get into our room and stay there," said Peter. "I don't think those blokes liked us at all."

"They'll get theirs after the match," said Jet. "I can wait."

Chapter Twelve

THE GREAT MATCH

THE OVAL AT WILLALONG was fast filling to capacity when Peter and Jet arrived the next morning a little after eleven o'clock.

The people of Central Districts took their football very seriously, and the Junior teams received as much interest as the Seniors. Because of the somewhat restricted area from which each town or area would have to get its players, the Juniors represented the recruiting source for the future main team. The boys were watched with critical analysis as future hopes for the welfare of their football club.

Bill Langforth had no desire to upset his boys by too many last-minute instructions, but he issued a warning in the final briefing.

"Kyeema has two dark horses," he told the team. "It's over six weeks since we played them last. In that time they have gained a couple of sixteen-year-old fellows who are pretty good—Clarrie Reddin and Mick Coffey."

"Oh no!" said Jet and Peter together.

The coach turned on them. "You know them?" he asked.

"We ought to. We had a terrible fight with them when they were in the shearing team at Yullamooloo, and last night they tried to do Jet and me over, with a gang. Set after us in the main street."

"That's very bad," said Langforth. "Once we let this match develop into a grudge match, we're done. I'll give you both a warning, Devlin and Mercedes, that if you are in any way responsible for any incidents, I'll take you both off. If you want a fight, you can have it in the ring at the Police Boys' Club after the game, not on the football field."

"What do we do if they go for us?"

"You shouldn't have to ask that sort of question. You play the ball all the time. Keep an eye out for any dirty work, but play the ball not the man. Contrary to what some of you fellows think, umpires have eyes, and it won't take the ump very long to see what's going on. They'll probably both be playing ruck. If things get too willing, leave it to me; I'll put a man on to cover you. In the meantime you're big enough and in good enough condition, Devlin, to trade good, solid, honest bumps. If you aren't, you shouldn't be playing. Young Jet is agile enough to be able to keep out of trouble, and I doubt if there's anyone in the district or anywhere else able to stop him."

Just the same, the boys could see that Langforth was worried. The play in the finals in these matches was always rugged enough, with intertown or inter-district jealousies intruding, and if a deep-rooted dislike between players intruded into the game, it could upset all the careful training of the past season.

Langforth decided to wait till the game settled down, so that he could see where Reddin and Coffey ended up and take steps accordingly.

The Daniel Creek Demons ran out on to the field through the usual mass of blue-and-gold streamers, to the hysterical screams of the teenage girls from the local high school.

Peter had had a dreadful feeling in the pit of his stomach most of the morning, but once they ran on to the ground this left as if by magic. As he looked at the field and the members of the team moving around, Peter became conscious only of the game and his desire to get on with it.

Kyeema delayed their entrance to such a degree that they nearly overdid it and had the umpire send in for them, but just as he was about to do so, they ran out on to the field. Their red-and-white colours contrasted vividly with the blue-and-gold of the Daniel Creek Demons.

Impatient at the late arrival of the other

side, the umpire had them lined up for inspection and ordered them off to their places in very short time. It seemed to Peter that he had barely enough time to reach the centre circle before the ball was bounced.

Peter was taking first knock. It was a good one and went straight out to Jet, who kicked it up to the half-forwards in a flash. Peter, however, was not interested.

Seconds after he had punched the ball on, Coffey, the opposing ruckman, leapt right across the circle and shirtfronted him. The umpire, with his eyes already following the flight of the ball, was unsighted, and though he looked back and saw the fallen boy, he did not blow his whistle.

For a moment the wind was knocked completely out of Peter and he lay gasping, unable to rise.

Langforth, taken aback by this sudden onslaught in the first seconds of the game, recovered quickly enough to send the second knock ruckman on the ball while the trainers carried Peter towards the back line.

"Look out for Coffey," the runner warned the relief. "He's going to play the man."

Peter soon recovered his wind and struggled to his feet as quickly as he could, furious that he had been skittled so early in the game. As he did so, the ball made a quick passage down the field towards him. He had lost his anger now, and this was replaced with a steely determination not to be outwitted again, but to reach the ball at all costs and boot it in the right direction.

Coffey had moved up into the goal square, where he stood supremely confident, waiting for the ball to reach him.

As he did so, Peter made a whirlwind rush. Coffey was bumped sprawling as his finger-tips touched the ball, which Peter snatched from under his nose and booted well back over the halfback line.

The crowd, enjoying the personal conflict, gave a great cheer, while Peter had the satisfaction of seeing the ball drop safely into the arms of a blue-and-gold player.

It was here that Jet began to show his brilliance, which dazzled his opponents and the crowd for the rest of the quarter, and assisted in bringing four of the goals, one by Jet from an impossible angle.

Realising that Peter had now recovered, and not wishing to lose the Devlin-Mercedes combination, Langforth quickly moved him back to the ruck, and the result caused dismay and despondency among the Kyeema players.

Nevertheless, a match with so much cut and thrust in it right from the beginning had to slacken off sooner or later, and by half time, the Kyeema team had recovered some of their lost ground, and trailed by only one goal.

"Remember," Langforth entreated his crowd of weary footballers when they came in for the break, "you have two more quarters to go. Now go and freshen up. I'm not going to talk to you too much."

The third quarter was almost a disaster for the Demons as the Kyeema team piled on six goals. Do what they could, there was no piercing the strong defence when Coffey and Reddin were there. Peter dropped right back and managed to stop the whole thing from becoming a rout, and it was evident that Daniel Creek were on the defensive.

Langforth refused to become upset. He ordered the captain to run as a loose man, and decided to keep Peter on the ball as long as he could.

It paid dividends. The old Devlin-Mercedes combination began to come into its own again, much to the delight of the crowd, who saw the five goal deficit of the third quarter gradually converted to a one goal lead.

Peter, by now, had the measure of both Coffey and Reddin, and the crowd knew it. On one occasion he ducked out of a deliberate sandwich so that both his opponents collided and fell to the ground. On another, Reddin tried a shirt-front in the ruck, but this time Peter flung himself sideways, with the result that the fellow went sprawling on the grass, while the rest of the field were metres away with the ball going in the direction of the goal.

At that stage, it apparently penetrated the mind of the Kyeema coach that they were playing the wrong game, for a runner came out with instructions to both Coffey and Reddin, and they again began to play the ball instead of the man. The result was immediately apparent.

A quick snap at the posts by one of the Kyeema players brought up a goal, and with only time on to go, the scores were even.

Peter's feet felt like lead, his arms were bruised, his tongue seemed to be sticking to the roof of his mouth and he would have preferred to have laid down and died.

Jet saw this, and while the ball was out of play for a second, he ran past Peter and yelled, "Always said you were only a blooming boy."

"Damn him," Peter muttered. "Damn him. I'll show him." Jet had struck home effectively.

The ball came towards him. He jumped and punched it into space. Jet was there. Coffey was bearing down on him.

"Back!" yelled Peter, and Jet instinctively flicked the ball back so quickly that Peter almost lost it. He recovered and booted the ball with all the strength he had.

It was a colossal kick from an impossible distance. As the huge crowd tensed for the outcome, the siren blew, a split second after the ball flew straight and true between the big posts.

There was pandemonium from the crowd and a yell of delight from the Demons. Jet and Peter were carried shoulder-high off the ground.

Chapter Thirteen

THE GOAT BUSINESS

THE NEXT WEEK WAS a great anticlimax for both boys. It was compensated for, perhaps, by the fact that Harry Stewart was in the seventh heaven of delight, not only with their win but with the equal success of the Senior Team.

"Don't ask him for Yullamooloo," May Stewart said to the boys. "He'd probably give it to you—and then I'd be without a home."

"Not while I'm around," said Jet, surprisingly.

It was the first time that Jet had allowed himself any statement indicating that he had any affection for anyone or anything. On a sudden impulse the woman put her arm round him and said impulsively, "Jet, it's wonderful to know I now have three sons here."

Peter was about to protest in jest about being left out, but as he looked at Jet he saw that there were tears in the other boy's eyes.

Mr Stewart also took the cue. "It's mighty fine to have another footballer in the family."

To their surprise. Jet rushed from the room.

"Hey, what did I say?" queried Mr Stewart.

"Nothing that wasn't right, Harry dear. Jet's just found a little bit more of himself."

"You're pretty nice people," said Peter. "I wonder if you know how nice you are."

Stewart threw back his head and laughed heartily. "That's pretty good of you, kid, but remember we only treat people at Yullamooloo the way they deserve."

"Thanks," said Peter, "I'll try to remember that too."

Tim came in at that moment with a weird contraption in his arms.

"Out!" said Mr Stewart. "I told you never to bring your inventions into this house."

"You'll enjoy this one," said Tim. "Dedicated to Messrs Stewart, Devlin, and Mercedes—footballers."

"What is it?" asked Mrs Stewart, keeping her distance.

"An automatic football blower-upper," said Tim, "specially designed for inflating footballs."

"Never," said Mr Stewart. "You'll either blow them out or pump them so hard they'll be useless."

"Not this one, father, dear father," said Tim, in the usual mocking tone he reserved for him. "I've learnt a lesson from Peter. It automatically cuts off at the right pressure."

He produced a number of deflated footballs.

"Not in the house," warned his mother. "Outside, please."

Tim looked hurt.

"This one works."

"So does your bale loader, but it had its teething trouble, you remember."

"Come on, Tim," said Peter. "I have faith in your new invention. I'll even stand alongside you while you work it."

"What confidence," said Tim, mockingly still. "Just the same I appreciate it. Come on."

They went outside and the gadget was put into operation. Astonishingly it worked right from the start.

Mr Stewart was surprised but impressed.

"We'll present it to the football club. They will doubtless find it very useful. Thanks, son."

"Genius wins through," replied Tim, with a self-satisfied smirk.

Old Joe Wilson was still working away in the shearing shed, but as the number of sheep in the holding paddocks grew less, both the boys realised that he would soon be leaving.

It had been a great satisfaction to them to have Joe nearby. This applied particularly to Jet, who was more inclined to listen to Joe than to anyone else.

The old man was not unaware of this, but he

proceeded cautiously. He knew that Jet was at the cross roads as regards his future, but he also knew that one incautious word at this time might push the boy to a decision which could be disastrous for him.

Peter managed to catch Joe on one occasion when Jet was away in some distant part of the station, doing some repairs with Les.

"What do you think is going to happen to Jet?" Peter asked him quite directly.

The old man gave his usual hitch of his trousers, scratched his head, and sat down on a small oil drum.

"How should I know? I ain't God."

"You certainly don't give me the impression you are, but you know Jet as well as any."

"Knowing the boy doesn't mean that I know what's best for him."

"It helps."

"Maybe, but in this case he's so mixed up he doesn't know where he's headed either. For that matter, what about you?"

"I don't think it matters about me. I can still educate myself. As a matter of fact I've been doing some extra study in my spare time. Mr Williams helped me get the books and things from the local high school. There's a future here for me if I want it and I can move over to the big house whenever I want to."

"So can Jet."

"That's the very point. Will he want to? He's swinging that way at present. I know that. The thing is, if he does, will he be doing the right thing?"

"Why not? He's got a future here with Mr Stewart. What else is there—to be a drifter on the edge of a country town for the rest of his life?"

"It doesn't follow—plenty of people with Aboriginal blood have fitted into the community."

"Depends on how much Jet is identified with his old man and that lot. Jacky Windmill doesn't want him any more. He knows he made a mistake when he brought the boy back from the city and he wants the boy to get a bit more out of life than he has."

"It's mighty complicated, isn't it?"

"Yep. It's something you can't hurry along, son. What happens to Jet will not depend on something sudden, but on how things go from day to day—how much he gets on with you, with the boss and the missus. Don't try to force it."

"We haven't got far, have we, Joe?"

"You never can get far when you're discussing Jet and the people he springs partly from. Understand him as much as you can, son, but don't play God."

Peter walked away, turning it all over in his mind and as confused as ever. He knew he was going to be very sorry when old Joe moved on.

That this might be delayed, however, was indicated a day or two later when Mr Stewart announced that they were going to have a goat drive.

"I thought you were going to get the shooters out," said Jet.

"I was, but I've had a bit of good news. The Northern Pastoral Company have been in touch with me and they are after every goat they can get."

"What for?"

"A new market has opened up in one of the Middle East countries for goat meat. I've got a proposition to put to you two fellows and old Joe, if he will stay. We'll go into business together. If you like to set up a team to get the goats out, we'll deduct all costs from the proceeds, and you can share the rest."

The plan would have appealed to any boys. It was a good exercise in station management, but as they discussed the probable costs and possible profits, Jet for the first time began to realise his own inadequacies in regard to working out the business problems associated with such a venture.

This, more than anything else, broke down the final reserve between the boys. For once Jet was in a world in which he had to depend on Peter for the answer to the questions.

At the same time this annoyed the boy, and he did his best to follow the calculations that the others were doing. He had been a reasonably good scholar before he left the city, but had developed a contempt for the process of learning and the results of it. During his association with Peter this attitude had been slowly changing.

Already his speech, by pure imitation, had greatly improved. Peter felt that initially the boy had developed ungrammatical speech not because he had not learnt to speak properly, but because if he had used different speech, it would have placed him on another level from those with whom he had been consorting during the past few years.

Chapter Fourteen

THE MYSTERIOUS MR SYMON

IT WAS ABOUT THIS TIME that the mysterious Mr Kevin Symon appeared at the station. He arrived one day in a Toyota four-wheel-drive vehicle, much the worse for wear and filled with all sorts of gear in the back.

Apart from a, "This is Mr Symon," from Mr Stewart, in a brief introduction to Peter, no reason for the man being on the property was given. Peter noticed, however, that he and Mr Stewart were very much in each other's company and he had been given the best bedroom in the house.

Symon was a tall man with a weather-beaten face and greying hair brushed carelessly back over his head, a moustache of the same colour which dropped down on each side of the man's mouth, blue eyes, a very pleasant voice, and a good sense of humour. Peter thought he was aged about forty-five.

He came and went from the station informally and returned at odd intervals to stay a day or two before disappearing again. There was conjecture at the shearing shed as to what he was and what he was doing. Peter and Jet came across the marks of the tyres of his Toyota quite often in their search for the ever-moving herds of goats, and on occasions even saw the dust rising from the place where he was taking his vehicle. Generally, however, he kept well out of their way.

"Could be an investigator," suggested Joe, "but I ain't heard that Harry has been losing any stock."

Jet came on traces of where the man had camped and noticed certain things—a pile of chipped stones, the handle of a broken hammer. He did not mention anything to Peter, as he did not think them important.

However, Peter had been observant too. It seemed to him that Mr Symon was acting suspiciously. Whatever he was doing had the blessing of Mr Stewart, but Peter, being a boy, was naturally curious.

At every opportunity he gave the Toyota an inspection in case the contents should indicate Mr Symon's purpose, but the back was always covered with a tarpaulin.

However, one thing he did notice—there was always a hammer lying on the front seat.

Then the penny dropped—hammer—geologist.

Down at the shed he mentioned this to Joe.

"Could be," said Joe, "could be."

"What's a geologist?" asked Jet.

"A bloke that pokes round to find minerals," said Peter. "He takes samples of rocks—breaks them open to see what's inside."

"Oh," said Jet, "that's what the stones were I found at a campsite of his."

"Where was that?"

"Out in Yulgana paddock not far from the ranges. I'll show you next time we go out after the goats."

In the meantime the goat business was flourishing. A nearby abattoir was having a slack period and was glad to have anything that would keep the killing floors going. Mr Stewart managed to bargain what he considered would be a fair price. To him, almost anything that a goat brought was a fair price, when he considered that with the price of bullets and the wages of hunters, he would be well out of pocket if he had to pay to have them exterminated.

The company exporting the meat did not buy the goats on-the-hoof but was willing to pay sixteen cents a kilogram for the carcasses, dressed. The average dressed goat weighed over thirteen kilograms. The end result was that Harry Stewart was covering the cost of transport and labour, and coming out even, the boys and old Joe were making a profit out of each goat, and Yullamooloo was being freed of its goats, which were destroying fine feed, at no cost whatever to Harry Stewart. It was an operation in which everyone was happy—except the goats.

As they cleared paddock after paddock of the animals, Peter and Jet went further and further afield, until they were spending a considerable time in the range of hills to see if there were any animals to be picked up there.

They often saw Mr Symon's four-wheel-drive parked at the foot of some cliff. Sometimes they caught glimpses of the owner working high up in the hills above them. It was apparent that he was following the ridges.

Peter could see that Jet was becoming more and more interested in the man's progress, and made every excuse to go out to the edge of the range where Symon was operating.

This appeared strange to Peter, as it was in this very area, some time before, that Jet had refused to come, and there had been so much fuss when they flushed the sheep out of Devil's Gorge.

One day Jet suggested that they load the bikes with provisions and spend a day or so camping in the paddocks.

"That way," he explained to Mr Stewart,

"we can be on the job all the time we would otherwise take going backward and forward. I know where there is plenty of water."

Peter was happy to agree with the plan. They took sleeping bags and a supply of rations, and moved to the outer edges of the plain country. Again, however, Jet gradually travelled back towards the Minn-narie Range.

"We've pretty well covered this area," Peter protested. "We're not doing well here at all."

"Okay," said Jet. "You go where you want. I'll stop off here."

They were now close enough to the range to be able to hear, from somewhere, the grinding of the motor of a four-wheel-drive. Jet looked towards the range and Peter, following his gaze, found himself looking at Devil's Gorge.

"Jet," he said, realisation coming, "you're a dope. Why didn't you tell me. You're frightened that Mr Symon will find the gorge and your place, aren't you?"

As he said it, Peter realised that he had made a slip. Jet was quick to notice.

"You know!" he said, not so much as a question, but as a statement—but it was a disconcerting mode of speech he had, against which Peter had no defence.

"Yes, Jet, I know. I found the hidden place you were so worried about. I went in, but when I found where I was I turned back to make sure no one else found it. I never even looked inside the caves."

"No, you wouldn't. You understand more than I think, sometimes. Was that why you came after me down at the stockmen's hut?"

"Partly. I don't like it when you're in trouble."

"If Symon finds the place, everything will be lost. There will be nothing—not even us."

"Let's divert him then," said Peter. "Let's find a way up the ranges where he's working, and turn him away from the place."

With Jet leading, they rode back along the hillside to where they had heard the Toyota a little while before. In due course they picked up some tyre tracks and after a closer examination Jet pointed to the way the vehicle had gone.

Symon was driving in low gear and after some time the boys caught sight of the slow-moving vehicle. The driver did not hear them as they closed up on him from behind.

When it was apparent that he was stopping, they cut their engines, and dropped back, so that he would not see them.

Ahead, the roar of the motor also ceased, and a few minutes later they heard the "tap-tap" of the hammer on rock.

They walked along quietly till they were both standing behind the man, who had his back to them and was examining the rock face.

"Blast," he said, turning. "What are you doing here?"

"It's a free country," said Peter. "We're looking for goats. What about you; found any good samples lately?"

To their surprise, Symon laughed.

"Harry told me you can't keep secrets long in this part of the world. You guessed."

"No guess about it, Mr Symon. You were careless, always leaving your hammer on the front seat and bits of broken-up stone over the countryside."

"Nearly half a million hectares," groaned Symon, "and you had to find just the spot where I threw away some useless samples."

"Are you finding anything?" asked Jet.

"That's a question I'm not replying to. Now shall we all go about our original business?"

Jet refused to be put off.

"You're wasting your time round here, Mr Symon. Why don't you try some of the other ranges?"

"Are you a geologist, young fellow?"

"No. But my mob know this country pretty well. I've heard them say that if we get minerals in this part of the world, it will be in the rusty country on the other side of the valley."

Symon did not rise to the bait.

"That may be so, but I'm trying this part out first. Thanks for the information. Goodbye."

The boys turned and walked back to their bikes. Symon watched them go, and then continued with his investigation.

They moved carefully downhill and made camp in a small gorge which had a pool of deep fresh water at its far end. Later in the day they heard the vehicle go by.

"Symon has come down from the hills," said Peter. "He's making towards Devil's Gorge."

They made tea, and after talking for a while, settled to sleep for the night.

Peter awoke once during the night. Jet was not there. He was too tired to think about it and fell off to sleep again. When he awoke in the morning, Jet was snoring nearby.

Strangely enough, Jet was quite content to move back to the plain that day. Two days later they returned to the homestead, after penning a considerable number of goats in one of the paddocks. Old Joe took a transport and Les and Tim went with him to help with the loading.

They returned later in the day. Kevin Symon was with them.

They watched him talking with Stewart.

"Can't understand it," the boys heard him say. "The Toyota broke down and I just couldn't get her going again. I carry plenty of spares, but she had me beaten."

"Why didn't you radio in?"

"Couldn't. The battery appears to have collapsed."

"Did you have to walk far?"

"No further than I wanted to. I saw the dust from the transport coming out that way, and so I lit a signal fire. Old Joe came over and picked me up."

Peter looked at Jet, but his face showed no flicker of interest in what they were saying.

Kevin Symon saw the boys.

"You've got a pair of nosey-parkers, Harry. They must have followed me all the way to Minn-narie."

Stewart called the boys over.

"What was the big idea?"

"We were looking for goats and found Mr Symon," said Jet.

Harry Stewart looked at the boy keenly to see if he was trying to be funny. Jet's face was full of innocence.

"That's a fact," said Peter. "Lucky we didn't round him up and put him on the transport."

"Quit hedging," said Stewart. "Last time Jet was out that way he had a sudden fit of blindness in the aeroplane, and then refused to go out and bring in the sheep that escaped to Devil's Gorge. Now it appears, young Devlin, that you've joined the tribe. What the hell's the matter with the place?"

"Sacred Ground?" said Symon. "When I

found the wagon unsound, I did a bit of exploring by foot. It paid dividends, Harry. I also found an old ceremonial area too—sacred stones and caves full of remarkable paintings. The area will have to be preserved, of course. It's probably one of the most remarkable finds for many years. I've got a lot more to tell you, but we have two pairs of long ears listening in."

The men turned and entered the house. Peter turned to where Jet had been standing but he had disappeared. Thoughtfully Peter walked back to the bungalow.

Chapter Fifteen

SHORT, SHARP, BUT IMPORTANT

HARRY STEWART AND KEVIN SYMON were in the homestead living-room sitting at a small table, having a drink. Out of sight, below the window ledge, Jet crouched.

"If the vehicle hadn't broken down, Harry old boy, I'd never have stumbled on it. But as I knew I had to wait, I started to scratch around. I found this great gorge. I believe you call it Devil's Gorge. Harry, if my early checking proves right, I landed on one of the biggest mineral deposits of its kind in the country. The sooner you can get into town and lodge a claim, the better it will be for you. You'd better get the whole area pegged carefully at once. There'll be a rush once the news gets around, as it must do sooner or later."

"As good as that?" asked Stewart.

"Harry, it's fantastic. You'll end up with a big mining town there. Nothing can stop it. The whole gorge and hill will go eventually, and even the remarkable caves I found. We can preserve them for a while—ten years perhaps—but someone will bring pressure to bear and they'll go too. You'll be a wealthy man, Harry, and what's more, we need this sort of development. It will provide employment for thousands."

"I'll get to work arranging a development team," said Stewart. "It's a pity though that it had to be the Minn-narie Range and that gorge in particular."

"Oh, why is that?"

"The Aborigines regard it as a special place. In their eyes we shouldn't even go there, let alone dig it all up."

Jet felt shaken to the very depths of his soul. His worst fears were becoming a dreadful reality.

Peter heard him enter the bungalow. He waited a moment and then walked to the boy's room.

"It's finished," said Jet, "finished. It's all over."

"You mean the Sacred Ground?"

"More than that. The whole lot. Gone."

Peter turned away. There was so little he could say. As he did so, he heard Jet giggle—a hysterical giggle, a ridiculous giggle coming at this time.

"I put his ruddy bus out of action to stop him finding the gorge. Because I put his ruddy engine out, he finds the gorge. Very funny."

The boy stood still for a moment and then rushed from the room, through the front door, and down towards the road leading to the escarpment.

Peter let him go. There was nothing to say. There was nothing he could do.

Chapter Sixteen

JET DISAPPEARS

THERE WAS MOVEMENT at the station, but not the sort of movement that the old poets had envisaged when they wrote about "the man from Snowy River." Harry Stewart and Kevin Symon went one way in the executive plane, and Les and Tim the other in the small plane in the direction of the Minn-narie Range.

Stewart had called Peter to him and told him the full details.

"You'd have to know sooner or later and it's best for me to be frank with you. At present we've got to put a tight curb on all our tongues. Where's Jet?"

"I haven't seen him since last night," said Peter. "He shot through when he found that Mr Symon had found the gorge."

"I hope he doesn't do anything silly. If he goes to town and babbles this around, it can set things off before we're ready."

"That's the last thing he would do, Mr Stewart."

"Well, find him and make sure he doesn't. I'll see you later."

Peter examined the bike shed. None of the bikes was missing. He then went to look for old Joe.

Joe had seen the boy near the stockmen's huts but had not come close to him. Peter explained as much as he felt he could of the circumstances.

"Jet is still so uncertain as to which way his future leads that he sets great store on anything in regard to Aboriginal lore and so on," said Joe. "When they initiate them they drill something in pretty deeply."

Peter found it hard to keep the old man's mind on this matter, however, as he had just had news about the consignments of goats they had sent away.

"Reckon Peter that we'll divvy up about $800 between us. To me it's a nice little nest egg just for helping to get the consignments off and taking them to market; to you it's very handy, and to Jet it's a fortune."

"It was worth while, Joe, and a lot of fun working together. What are you planning to do next?"

"I'll stick around, Peter, for a bit. Mr Stewart doesn't want me to go. There's plenty to keep me busy round here for some time, in many ways. I'll earn my keep."

"That's fine, Joe. I'll report back after I've found Jet."

"You tried the gorge?"

"No. What makes you think he'll go there?"

"Just a hunch. There's a lot of his mob gone walkabout in the last week or so. Watch the skyline. I've noticed quite a lot of smoke."

"I thought that all went out years ago."

"Most did. Few of the Aborigines we know remember much of their original customs, but some do."

"Sounds a bit impossible, but I suppose you're right. Anyway I'll take your suggestion and go out to the gorge tomorrow, if I haven't found Jet before then. He hasn't taken a bike and it's at least fifty kilometres. He'd have a long walk."

"Not for him. He'd be there in a day."

Unfortunately, the next day Les needed Peter in the plane to help set up a base in the Ranges. Peter hoped that he might have the chance of moving into the gorge, but the only safe landing was about ten kilometres away.

They ran backwards and forwards all day in the small Cessna, taking out equipment and small drums of petrol.

"Can't overdo it," said Les. "This isn't a transport plane, but if we manage three or four drums a trip, it builds up and will save us having to bring the vehicles back here to refuel."

Les sensed Peter's worry about Jet, and on his request did a run over the gorge area, but they could see nothing.

It was not till the third day after Jet had disappeared that Peter could make his own plans to find the boy. Mr Stewart had taken the larger plane to Daniel Creek to finalise legal matters in regard to the mining claim. Les was doing a boundary run in the smaller plane and did not need Peter for this. Peter refuelled one of the bikes and as soon as the others had left set off for the gorge.

He was well equipped with food and water. It was just as well. About ten kilometres from the range he had a bad blowout of a rear tyre.

He was not very anxious about his predicament, but annoyed that such a thing had happened. For long-range trips they did not carry the usual walkie-talkie, but a powerful radio which fitted on the tank and had a range of several hundred kilometres. For safety he had arranged a calling schedule with the station on the even two hours. As it was just after ten when the mishap occurred, he missed the calling time by a few minutes, and had to sit and wait till twelve before he made contact.

Mrs Stewart was looking after the radio at the homestead and had had her hands full, with the two planes in the air and the usual radio traffic of the station. When Peter's call came in, she replied that Les was still away with the plane, but as soon as he returned she would have him run out and drop a tyre.

Peter turned the radio off and after eating his lunch found a shady tree, sat down and went to sleep. It was three o'clock in the afternoon before Les came out with the truck. He had brought another bike.

"I've still got plenty of time to get out to the range," said Peter, "so I think I'll get moving."

He put the radio on to the other bike and set off. Unfortunately he was not to have a free run over the rest of the country, as the chain kept slipping off, and he had to spend time adjusting the back wheel. It was therefore much later in the afternoon than he expected before he reached the entrance to the gorge.

By now it was six o'clock, and so he took the opportunity to contact the station.

"I'm too late to scout around here in the remaining daylight," he reported. "I'll make camp, have a look round in the morning and come back bright and early."

Mrs Stewart was a little anxious.

"Are you sure you'll be all right, Peter?"

"Of course. What is there to worry about?"

"Nothing really, Peter, but I'll worry till you're back, just the same."

"You're like a mother," said Peter.

"Why not?" was the reply. "You're part of the family."

"Thanks," said Peter. "Thank you, Mrs Stewart."

It was good to know someone cared for him.

Before dark he had moved in to the gorge. He extracted his sleeping bag from the saddle-bag, wriggled into it, and dropped off to sleep very quickly in a small sheltered spot, where a patch of light soil provided a more comfortable resting place than most of the other areas.

Chapter Seventeen

WHICH WAY, JET?

PETER AWOKE A FEW HOURS later—not from discomfort, but because he had been disturbed by something. The night was very still and he strained his ears wondering what had jarred him back to consciousness. Then suddenly it came—a long low moaning sound, which lasted a second and then was gone. He strained his ears a little more.

The sound was repeated, and he heard a roaring sound—the same kind of sound that he used to make when he whirled a ruler round his head on a piece of string at school.

"It can't be," he reflected. "Not a real bull-roarer." Then faintly there came to his ears the sound of tapping sticks. The noise was coming from the direction of the caves and the Aboriginal ceremonial ground.

Peter had a small pocket torch which he had taken from the bike; it was part of the equipment in case of trouble at night.

Carefully he moved up the gorge. There was

a smell of smoke, which grew stronger as he moved through the narrow cleft he had found on his first visit there.

The noise increased, and he heard a strange chanting and saw ahead of him that the walls all around were illuminated by many fires. He switched off his torch and moved up quietly.

As he came out of the cleft, a remarkable sight greeted his eyes. A fire blazed in front of every cave, and in the centre another lit up the strange heaps of stones. Moving around the fires and casting weird shadows as they did so were twenty or more Aborigines.

They had cast off their clothing and were chanting as they stamped their way around the arena. One slim, pale form stood out. It was Jet.

To one side a small group of men were sitting, tapping sticks; a man was blowing a didgeridoo. Peter drew into the shadows and watched.

The meaning of what he saw was beyond Peter's comprehension, yet, almost against his will the boy felt a strange excitement as the rhythm of the movements before him, together with the rising pulse of the music, began to take a hold on him.

The sharp insistent tapping of the sticks found a thousand echoes from the strong, rugged, flame-lit walls of the gorge. Underneath, the deep, dull echoes of the didgeridoo rolled backward and forward, as if to convey that this was a Mystery—a mystery which he, Peter Devlin, would never understand.

Yet, with it all, the sound, the movement, the flickering fires, and the wild echoes from the high buffs around, merged into one unforgettable impression. For a moment Peter had the urge to tear off his clothes and join in the wild unfettered freedom of the dancers before him, and in another he knew that this was a world as forbidden to him as it was to the uninitiated. In this Jet was indeed the man he claimed himself to be; in this he, Peter, was indeed the boy.

How long he would have stood, how long this wild dancing would have continued Peter would never know, for suddenly the movement ceased, the tapping sticks died away, and the echoes of the didgeridoo faded.

Every movement was frozen. Standing to one side, a huge man with arms outstretched had in one movement erased the sound and stopped the movement. He moved with dignity to a large rock.

The rest, still motionless, regarded him in silence.

"It is no use," he said slowly and with dignity, and the echoes took his words and tumbled them around the gorge. "Soon all this will be gone and all of us with it."

"No," shouted one of the young men, and the echoes cried, "No, no, no," and died away.

"Who can stop the sun from rising?" asked the man. The rest regarded him with eyes from which all hope had faded.

Suddenly the deep, soft throbbing of the didgeridoo filled the gorge with its insistent, tragic call. All except the man on the rock dropped to the ground and the place was filled with the singing of the men in a low, oft-repeated but clear cry of lamentation.

"No," said Peter to himself. "No. This must not happen. Someone must understand."

He watched the huge man drop from the rock. From somewhere he picked up a full bottle of beer and knocking the top off stood beyond the fires and poured the contents down his throat.

When he had finished he flung the empty bottle into the mouth of one of the caves crying out in a loud voice, "There is nothing sacred for us any more."

There was no sound now. The droning had died away, the singing had ceased. One by one the men stood up, shook themselves as if rising from a sleep, and moved to the mouth of the caves. Soon there came the tinkle of other bottles being broken against the rocks.

Peter turned and stumbled back down the cleft. He had seen enough. Indeed he had seen too much; it was almost so unreal that surely it could not have happened.

After a search the boy found his sleeping place and flung himself down on it. Though he felt he could never sleep with this wild, unreal scene so vividly etched on his mind, in time, sleep he did. His dreaming was disturbed by the stark beauty of the dancing he had seen and the evil that had followed.

He did not waken until the sun was well up. In the daylight the events of the night before seemed quite improbable.

There was no sound from the gorge but, as he watched, he saw emerging from the area a group of Aborigines. He recognised some of them, but there were many he did not know. He stood still while they, unaware of his presence, lurched off down the gorge.

Jet was not among them. Peter waited until the sound of the men's progress had died away, and then cautiously re-entered the narrow cleft to the ceremonial area.

The rising sun had filled the place with a golden glow. Only the embers of the fires of the night before remained to prove that it had really happened.

For a moment he felt that the place was empty but, looking towards the main fire, he saw a slim form lying on the ground. It was Jet.

For a moment Peter feared he was dead. He ran forward. The boy had dressed himself, but lay still and on his face. Peter knelt down beside him and raised him in his arms.

"Jet! Jet!" he cried. "Are you all right?"

Two brown eyes looked up at him. For once there was no defiance, or courage, or indeed any expression on the boy's face, except perhaps a blank bewilderment.

"Jet," said Peter gently. "Come on, boy. You're all right, aren't you?"

"Peter, it doesn't mean anything any more; it's finished. All finished."

Jet spoke softly and gravely. He seemed to be in a state of shock.

"No, it's not finished, Jet. It is only finished if everyone gives up—the Aborigines and the Europeans."

"And me?"

"You're a bridge, Jet. You share two worlds; you shouldn't be ashamed of either."

Jet did not reply. He looked at the ashes of the fires.

"I'm only a kid, Peter."

Peter shook the boy.

"No, Jet. When I watched you last night I suddenly felt that what you have been saying all the time was true—that you were a man."

For the first time Jet lost his tenseness.

"So you saw everything, Peter?" asked Jet.

"Yes, the good and the bad. Come on, man. You're cold and lying here won't do you any good."

Jet rose to his feet.

"Come," said Peter, "let's go down to my camp."

For a moment Peter felt Jet was going to refuse to move. Instead he moved up the gorge towards the caves. Peter followed him.

They came to the mouth of the largest cave. The early morning sun shone right into the place lighting up the walls. Jet pointed. The great painted symbols of the past were displayed in all their glory. The heap of broken beer bottles at their base seemed insignificant.

For a moment the two boys stood, both overawed by the wonder of what they saw.

"Come on," said Peter gently. "If you and I can understand, others can. This will be safe enough."

They turned, walked past the blackened and dead camp fires, down through the cleft, and then into the main gorge beyond.

In close communion they walked back into the world that awaited them.